The World is Around You, but You are in Your Car

William M. Trently

iUniverse, Inc.
New York Bloomington

The World is Around You, but You are in Your Car

iUniverse books may be ordered through booksellers or by contacting:

iUniverse
1663 Liberty Drive
Bloomington, IN 47403
www.iuniverse.com
1-800-Authors (1-800-288-4677)

Because of the dynamic nature of the Internet, any Web addresses or links contained in this book may have changed since publication and may no longer be valid.

ISBN: 978-1-4401-4283-3 (pbk)
ISBN: 978-1-4401-4284-0 (dj)
ISBN: 978-1-4401-4285-7 (ebk)

Printed in the United States of America

iUniverse rev. date: 5/21/2009

I was driving around aimlessly with no purpose or sense of teamwork in my car jealous of the guy in the Porsche cruising alongside my beat-up Hyundai when I ran a red light causing two cars to screech their brakes and rushed into a drive-through to get super-sized burgers and Coke which I pounded down and threw the garbage out the window as I listened to suicide bomb updates on the radio and searched for someone to blame or take to court for my own inadequacies but after all was said and done pulled over and got out of the comfort of the automobile to look around and saw that the world was around me.

WMT

Contents

Thank you to the following: Michael Pavuk for grammar foundations; Stanley Evans for instilling confidence; David Trently for his early support and typing; Kelley Conway and Dr. Peter Braseth for their critical feedback; Alice Peck for her expert editing; Bertha, Jennie, and Devin for their support and patience; and William J. and Evelyn Trently for being great parents.

PREFACE

I had often found conversations about current events to be inadequate—mere sound bites and fragmented random declarations thrown about with no anchor. There was so much more that first needed to be said as a prerequisite foundation, a common understanding from which to move forward. How could anyone discuss anything from taxes to military strategy without first addressing deeper issues? How could we understand why many people throughout the world were driven to commit acts of terrorism against us if we did not first explore more profound ideas about ourselves, far beneath the superficial? This book provides pieces of the foundation, the use of which can transform daily discussions so these become more fruitful, helping all of us make a better world.

The education, experiences, and personal interests of a common person living in the States are my only qualifications to write this book. I contribute the small voice of this short story to the world's ongoing conversations.

INTRODUCTION

The World is Around You, but You are in Your Car is a work of fiction wrapped around a kind of essay that describes an American problem—the **relentless pursuit of the perfect life**—and its negative consequences that adversely affect progress and behavior toward the rest of the world. "I want it, and I want it now," with its shortage of self-restraint, has been taken to levels not reached before, and the insidious ramifications are eye-opening, such as the easy disposability of people or principles if these should obstruct the path to the perfect life, or the mental depression from the strains of struggling to keep up with the neighbors, or the isolation from reality as people become more and more comfortable in their plush living rooms and cars.

The tale brings history's great philosophers together to sound an alarm and talk about ways to slow the relentless pursuit. They have already debated the relevant issues with each other; here in this story, their role is only to inform us of their conclusions. They discuss the external and internal controls that restrain the pursuit, agreeing that internal control, involving self-regulation of the individual, is more effective and desired than external, primarily because of its greater conduciveness to freedom, the crown jewel of this civilization. Historically, religion has played a large role in internal control and, when broadly and more accurately defined than the common notion, could be used to rein in the pursuit. Under this scheme, it would be up to each person to find something spiritual on which to hold as he or she makes the journey through life, for there are many paths from which to choose. For those persons who could not subscribe to any of the established religions, an honest and mature bottom-line system is humbly presented as merely one example of many alternatives. The object of the game is to emphasize internal restraint more than ever so that the "freedom experiment" has a better chance of succeeding.

The World is Around You also brings out two other ideas of particular interest. First, it follows that if a society chooses to cherish internal restraint, it must clarify the rules about what is and is not appropriate regarding religion in the public square. As Plato sets out to do this, he gives us a new way to define "god" that could be acceptable to even the atheist for use in the community domain. Second, note that Byron Dink is like many human beings when he laments that, despite a profound childhood desire to do something significant to make the world a better place, he felt he had not yet done anything. In Kierkegaard's suggestion of a common mission for all Americans, perhaps all of us could find something that would bind people closer together and provide our lives with a higher purpose, motivating us to action.

Since the story is fictitious, I have taken the liberty to bend and twist some of the descriptions of Portsmouth, but the overall ambiance of the city is intact.

A final introductory remark: here as we dwell in the first decade of the twenty-first century, it is useful to not only look behind and to the sides, but also ahead into the future when history is interpreted more accurately after time has passed and dust has settled and emotions of the moment have subsided, giving way to objective clarity. With this in mind, we may proceed to Part One.

PART ONE
THE SHORT HISTORY OF THE U.S.

September 11, 3000 CE
Student sitting on campus bench reads newly-published (circa June 3000), critically-acclaimed college textbook.
Student looks up, waves to approaching second student.
Second student: "What are you reading?"
"*The Short History of the United States*—for my sociology class."
"Cool."
Excerpt is graciously reprinted below, with permission, making up the remainder of this first chapter.

*

People everywhere, from the beginning of human time, pursued wants. They wanted food, water, and shelter. They wanted things not absolutely required for the most fundamental levels of survival, such as a recreational boat, home decoration, or CD player. They wanted intangibles like freedom, comfort, safety, and happiness.

The pursuit of wants, as always, meant different things to different people based on different personal desires. What was desired, why it was desired, when and how much was desired, and how intensely it was desired—all varied among people. One person liked ska while another preferred rock. An ascetic and a hedonist held very different views on what would be regarded as comfort. Another individual was happiest when reading a book on the beach, while someone else only when surfing the waves at the same beach. One girl wanted earnestly and enthusiastically to study for several hours a day, while a second girl could never sustain study beyond thirty minutes. One health-conscious person wanted to eat a maximum of one sweet each day as his only dessert. A second person craved at least five donuts, five cookies, and five candy bars daily. If it was discovered there were no donuts left in the pantry, the first person would not bother to make a special trip to the store to replenish the supply. The second person would undertake an emergency expedition.

The pursuit of wants also, as always, meant different things to different people based on limitations. The amount of money required to buy something could be limiting. Certain products might not be available everywhere. The amount of effort required to get something could be regarded by a minimally-motivated person as excessive, thus restricting its acquisition. People were limited by their mental and physical abilities—a consistent "D" student could not be valedictorian; a person with a broken leg could not compete in a marathon race.

People everywhere in the world, as always, wanted. There was a cartoon sketch of the generic human with an arm outstretched, hand gripping an object he desired, pointing with his other hand in another direction at some other object he also sought to obtain.

People living in the United States of America increasingly tended to pursue relatively more wants than people living elsewhere. "Americans," as they were called, had a great degree of personal freedom and abundance of resources, among other factors, that promoted this tendency. Those conditions provided a fertile ground from which individuals could desire and actually acquire more. The cartoon sketch was modified to portray the

American as a human with ten arms outstretched from one body, each hand holding a yearned-for object or pointing to one.

The culture of freedom in the United States allowed its inhabitants the opportunities to achieve personal goals and develop their own unique abilities to the fullest. The high degree of freedom was perhaps, arguably, the most significant factor influencing and provoking the greater wants. Having liberty to speak, assemble, create, inaugurate a club or charitable organization, pursue vacations, or start a new business opened doors to needs for additional materials and benefits. People from places that did not offer such freedom could only dream of those possibilities, while Americans could take their wishes a step further.

The United States, experiencing such a wealth of freedom, represented an experiment that might help determine for the world how much freedom could be safely bestowed upon humans before the privilege was abused, becoming counterproductive. Numerous scholars dubbed this "the freedom experiment."

Although there were many people who did not admire the ideas and actions of the Americans, there were many throughout the world who did. Many felt that a free society like the one in the United States, although imperfect, offered the greatest hope for a better future. People everywhere watched the experiment and, some of them, at times, adopted certain ideas from the Americans to use in their own unique homelands on the planet.

People saw that, in the United States, the greater wants led to much progress. As more individuals strived harder to get things, higher levels of progress resulted. Progress was the advancement of American society toward the status of being "better," which meant such conditions as being safer, more comfortable, healthier, more efficient and happier. It was the forging ahead to an elevated, more advanced stage.

Many inventions resulted, such as the television, the airplane, and the automobile. An abundance of medical advances arose. Astronauts landed on the moon. The middle class prospered.

Impressive strides forward were made in the realm of the arts. The civilization made it easier for handicapped persons to get around and participate more fully in society. Social, cultural, and political gains were observed. When people were allowed more freedom to pursue their wants, as they were in the United States, much positive progress resulted.

In time, however, there emerged a deep-seated negative development that infiltrated the American character. By about the year 2000, the pursuit of wants gradually evolved into what was eventually called by some individuals a "relentless pursuit of the perfect life," a derogatory description.

The word "relentless" meant showing or promising no abatement of severity or intensity. It portrayed conditions that were unrelenting, tending not to let up, slacken, soften, mollify, or yield. It was good to be relentless in the sense of not giving up, in being tenacious in seeking the attainment of goals, but it was not good when that seeking began to detract from progress and adversely affect people.

The word, "relentless," as used to describe the devolution stated above, connoted an insatiable selfishness where Americans were perceived as doing whatever it took to get what they wanted, regardless of harm rendered upon others. The pursuit of wants was unfettered, often at the unfair expense of other people who played by the rules and happened to be in the way.

Certainly, people all over the world, as always throughout history, periodically strayed toward and reached a relentless pursuit of wants. It was just that, in America, a previously unheard of, extreme, expanded level of this pursuit was actually arrived at, and was growing even more ferociously in intensity and frequency.

This represented something new in human development—a hyperrelentless pursuit of wants engaged in by larger numbers of ordinary human beings than ever before. Here was a negative development pertaining to the pursuit of wants greater in extent than anything experienced in previous times. In fact, the description, "pursuit *of the perfect life*," was inserted to emphasize the extreme magnitude. People had become so relentless that they expected, and demanded, perfection—that is, they expected to always get what they wanted. Their lives were supposed to be perfect. In the course of the cultivation of this attitude, they came to believe a flawless life—one without any inconveniences or obstructions—was absolutely owed to them, was automatically supposed to be had, was deservingly theirs to possess. If they were to fall short of getting what was wanted, they would lash out in anger and desperation.

The relentless pursuit of the perfect life was manifested by aloofness—a subtle, increasing distance laid down between people as they gradually lost sight of a societal team mission and genuine, sustained camaraderie. And as people hunkered down in the comfort of their own living rooms, they distanced themselves even further from the realities of the world outside.

The relentless pursuit of the perfect life was manifested by the development of a "disposable society," one in which you simply discarded a thing, person, or principle that happened to obstruct the path to that perfect life.

The relentless pursuit of the perfect life was manifested by a pervasive victimization, referring to a tendency by individuals to exaggeratedly claim they had been wronged and so required compensation, often finding no fault with their own shortcomings while blaming only others when things did not go their way. An assortment of rights and entitlements was demanded, responsibilities ignored, and self-indulgent lawsuits engaged in.

The relentless pursuit of the perfect life was manifested by a decline in health, as people experienced obesity and mental depression: obesity because they could not restrain their pursuit of food or physical inactivity, mental depression because they felt the strains of struggling to keep up with the neighbors in the pursuit of wants.

The more the pursuit of wants became the relentless pursuit of the perfect life, the greater the hindrance to society's progress.

The insidious ramifications caused a virulent drain on efficient societal advancement.

How could this society, increasingly burdened with the weight of the above-mentioned developments, have expected to continue its impressive record of accomplishments? How could it have sustained the capabilities required to transport a human to the moon again? Granted, the sheer size of the momentum of progress such a civilization had acquired over time was enough to successfully masque any negative downturn spawned from the relentless pursuit, especially in its primordial stages, but the dangers would become increasingly evident as the decline snowballed and began negating optimal outcomes as progress was greatly, noticeably slowed, ultimately threatening to destroy the American civilization.

To be sure, not all Americans were so vehemently engaged in a relentless pursuit, but more and more were being inducted into this movement, often in subtle ways of which they were not even conscious. Distressing trends were slowly permeating more and more people.

As scholars studied the collective character of the Americans, they could be assured, like Alexis de Tocqueville, that these were basically good people who were admired by many throughout the world. But these intellectuals would in the next moment have worried that this character was being tugged and twisted downward by increasingly stronger currents. They could begin to wonder if perhaps Dostoevsky's Grand Inquisitor was right when he complained God had made a big mistake in giving humans such high levels of freedom since they, by nature, could not handle it.

And the diminution of restraint unleashed by the relentless pursuit not only damaged the Americans domestically by pulling down progress, but also began affecting how they behaved toward the rest of the world, with grave consequences. The other nations could not continue, in the end, to suffer from America's relentless pursuit of the perfect life without pushing back so a new equilibrium could be reached.

PART TWO
PHILOSOPHERS

Football season neared. "My bets are on the Steelers this year," proclaimed Aristotle. "This'll be their season."

Socrates looked on, made a disgruntled face, and responded quickly, "Not a chance."

A waitress dropped a glass on the floor and it shattered, distracting the many breakfasters from their isolated conversations, or reveries, as the case might have been. The small restaurant in Portsmouth, New Hampshire was filled to capacity and was very lively this day.

Imagine if the world's greatest minds—or at least the ones that are described in the encyclopedia volumes—were liberated from the pages of history and brought together into the United States, sometime in September of the year 2008, when summer weather was winding down and fall was preparing to emerge.

Those human beings who were honored by the rest for having discovered or developed some new philosophical trend, for coming up with original thoughts, for having dragged something fresh into the collective warehouse of human ideas ... imagine these outstanding contributors together and alive again on earth.

Imagine if, after each passed away from the confines of earth, these philosophers continued to live somewhere else where observation of human development up to the present era was possible. They would have seen man's history unfurl; in their possession would be the ability to observe all events while having available the world's ever-growing knowledge.

They would have also acquired the technological advances to assist immensely in their observations. They would have discontinued using the abacus in favor of the calculator, although perhaps some would have stubbornly protested the former's "premature expiration date," since they, as many humans, were often initially prone to reluctance in breaking with old traditions and technologies.

And imagine that since they would have learned so much more than ordinary people by this unique surveillance, with time's passage many of their original ideas, formed on earth ages ago, would have begun unraveling, and then reorganizing and growing until changes occurred. Those centuries-old prototypical words recorded on paper or papyrus, would experience alterations and evolve even further, finally being thrust into a common coalescence with the other thinkers' revisions, a fresh consensus concerning certain perceptions laboriously attained.

Do not infer that their original thoughts were unimportant, but realize that their ideas would have grown. This kind of transpiration may occur to many of us over the passage of time! Surely many an ordinary human disposed to recording personal thoughts has discovered changes or maturations when old childhood notes tucked away at the bottom of a mildewed box are resurrected and compared with present preoccupations, the differences wrought by time and experience.

It is normal to initially feel guilty of playing the role of manipulator with such revered people's words, but it is important to remind oneself that different times have different ideas of what is "in," what is trendy, and what is regarded as true. To move from one era to another is to alter the vantage point and cultural context, which would affect one's point of view. If Bach composed during the Classical era, his music would have reflected the styles of those years—he would not have composed in the Baroque mode. He would have jumped from one paradigm to a completely different one. So how would the ideas of the philosophers change with the times?

Imagine that, despite past disagreements over philosophical observations, the great philosophers now were in concurrence about many of the ideas they dissected. Many, but not all—after all, it is difficult enough to imagine philosophers, being of the opinionated ilk, joining hands of agreement over just a few points, let alone an entire collection.

One specific idea the Great Minds now held in common stood out, proving to be the focus of the present tale: the search for and discovery of central ideas that could slow down the relentless pursuit of the perfect life. Here, they were in agreement.

Imagine if the dream of getting the philosophers together came true and they divulged these new ideas while they were in town visiting the world as it was known in 2008.

You would see Thales watch his unbounded water evaporate, Heraclitus' fire burn into Anaximene's air, and Pythagoras subtract his world of numbers until reaching a new common denominator.

Voltaire would cease hassling Leibniz. Nietzsche would apologize to John Stuart Mill for calling him a "blockhead" years ago. Students would quit saying they "can't understand Kant," for now his words would be more lucid than ever.

"It's hard to believe they'll be in town later this week," said John to his girlfriend Michelle, both college juniors. He held up a copy of the day's local newspaper, which declared about midway down the cover page, "Great Minds to Visit Portsmouth Saturday." John and Michelle were spending this Wednesday walking around downtown, hoping to catch glimpses of as many of the great thinkers as possible, if any of them happened to have arrived this early in the week.

The enthusiastic couple was now at the bookstore, browsing through some of the classics. Thomas More's *Utopia*, Aristotle's

Politics, Plato's *The Republic*, and Hobbes' *The Leviathan* were nesting, along with the others, among the various nooks of the bookshelves. *The Critique of Pure Reason*, by Immanuel Kant, reposed askew of the rest. Rene Descartes' *Essais Philosophiques* was torn at about the place you would first touch your finger at the book's top to pull it off the shelf. David Hume's *A Treatise of Human Nature* lay on its back, overlapping the shelf's precipice.

The early morning air was foggy and the narrow New England streets offered an occasional passerby. Carl Jenning, his skin tan and deeply weathered, occupied one of the sidewalk benches. He talked with Bob Lemieux, tall but stooped with poor posture, as they watched the pigeons feeding. Both were retired shipyard workers who enjoyed observing the activity downtown.

There was some excitement in the air about the philosophers, although in actuality not overly effervescent. After all, just how many humans could really be expected to be interested? There would be some, but not an overwhelming number. Carl could not understand the excitement, at any level, which seemed to have increased a bit since it was announced in the media that the great philosophers were to embark miraculously upon the city for one day's events. There was to be a small exhibit at the Sheraton, to be followed by a concert at the Music Hall. The rumor was that Beethoven was to appear for a performance of his Tenth Symphony. His Tenth Symphony! The Great Thinkers would attend the concert, as well as anyone else who had been lucky enough to have obtained a ticket.

Bob attempted to illuminate Carl as he explained: "Philosophy's supposed to be far removed from the goings-on of ordinary life. But nearly all of us have some philosophic views, whether we are aware of them or not! Like me, for instance, Carl. I have a whole philosophy on fly fishing ... "

Carl pointed to a brochure dropped on the ground by one of the tourists who visited the city. Carl said, "This here has a definition of philosophy. It says here ... wait a sec ... okay, here it is ... " He paused, then continued, " ... the organiz ... ation and clarification of ideas so we may test and weigh them in order to discover more definite conclusions closer to the truth."

Carl verbally staggered forward, reading the next line on the brochure: "By achieving this, we attain a more sig … nificant comprehension of the world; a systemic, coherent, consistent picture of all we know."

"That's it," said Bob. "It's really a perpetual search for truth! And the act of philosophizing is supposed to make our lives more satisfying." Carl looked a little puzzled.

"Let me tell you a story," ventured Bob. "There were two women who won a raffle in a grocery store. The prize was that each would be allowed to go on a fifteen-minute shopping spree. For fifteen minutes, each would wander through the store picking up merchandise that she wanted, and would be permitted to fill two large shopping carts. Everything that was placed into their carts would become theirs to keep … for free!

Now, fifteen minutes is not a lot of time, Carl. The first woman recognized this fact and so studied the entire store's layout of goods beforehand. She came to know exactly what she wanted, where it was, and how much time it would take to get each item. She then had a well-organized plan going into the spree.

The second woman did not spend any time preparing. She went into the spree blindly. Needless to say, she ended up getting less of what she really wanted, while the first woman successfully got everything she wanted."

Bob was trying to articulate that the person who takes the time to learn philosophy early in life will get more out of his subsequent life than the person who does not achieve this. Certainly, the latter person will proceed through his life, perhaps learning from personal experience by the time he is old much of what the former learned from the start, when he was young and studied philosophy. But the former holds the advantage of having much more time to understand *even more*, owing to the core knowledge obtained from the early philosophical indoctrination.

He therefore has the opportunity to augment his life experience over and above what the latter person experiences!

Bob moved along, "They say it makes for a more satisfying time of it in life."

Carl listened intently. He then continued to feed the pigeons. "And how is it that you come to know so much?" he asked.

"Well, actually I don't really know the particulars," admitted Bob, " … I just hear my niece and her college friends talking." A brightly dressed toddler escaped briefly from his parents and stumbled innocently where the pigeons had been feeding. The birds dispersed. Carl looked away.

It was said the great philosophers descended on Portsmouth because they heard the food was good and the scenic coastal views dramatic. At least that was the word circulating around town. Officially, according to their chief spokesman's press release, the explanation was given that "Although the food and scenery are indeed outstanding, there also was a certain degree of random choice involved. I believe it was Mr. Adam Smith who hurled a dart at a wall map highlighted with the finalists, the projectile coming closest to Portsmouth. Nevertheless, the important point is the message the thinkers will seek to impart, which is, in fact, intended to benefit all of the States."

And so all the great philosophers of human time were now huddled together in this small American city by the sea to present a symposium, open to the public, on Saturday! Maybe, to be accurate, it should be stated that *almost* all of them were in attendance—perhaps there would be a few who were indisposed or burdened with previously scheduled engagements that would not make it. Nevertheless, there was a quorum. And a few great scientists, artists, religious thinkers, as well as other renowned persons would also show up to lend a hand. Some arrived earlier that week. All would depart on Sunday, the day after the conference.

How lucky were the residents of this world to experience such an event as this, to have direct access to the expertise of so many of these special people! Such men were extremely rare. We were not likely to meet individuals like these anywhere in our lifetimes. For so many of them to be gathered together in one place at the same time was a true miracle, filled with unique opportunities.

Throughout the city the Great Minds roamed. Anaximander was robed in a two-piece pinstriped business suit, his curly hair covering part of his ears as he told a mailman in front of the historic post office, "Well, you can't appreciate nice sunny weather as much without also knowing the ice and snow of colder days." Immanuel Kant wore a "Moral Aid" T-shirt and his head donned a crew cut, as he strolled through Prescott Park.

John Stuart Mill and Jeremy Bentham walked downtown and were drinking Coke while Aristotle sipped an espresso. Zeno overheard Aristotle, the man who once described the Golden Mean, mumble something about the imbibition of beer being "good as long as you paced yourself. Man, pace thyself."

Descartes was reasoning his way through several games of chess, while Muhammad talked about his pilgrimage through New York's Central Park. Buddha sat with legs crossed on a chair at the laundromat, waiting patiently for his clothes to dry.

Thomas Hobbes played Ms. Pacman and was beaten five games in a row by Jesus, and in frustration insisted that Jesus was not a social being. Jesus just amicably laughed and walked away.

Here they were, representing a wide variety of views and a plethora of wisdom. They were a diverse lot, exhibiting a vast array of contrasting complexions, personal tastes, and abilities.

And the occupations they held during their lives on earth were as varied as their beliefs. Some were teachers; others were leaders of religious movements. Spinoza was a lens grinder by profession. Locke was a medical doctor. Mill was a magazine writer and member of Parliament. Many were scientists or mathematicians. Some were aloof from the everyday pursuits of common life; others were actively involved with society.

All of them had shared a common conviction that thoughtful examination of human views on life was important and worthwhile. They each wanted to define fundamental ideas and discover what it was that people based their knowledge about the world upon. They sought standards that could be used to arrive at sound, truthful judgments. They desired to find beliefs to which humans ought to adhere.

They worked diligently, often feverishly, in their toils. One could imagine the task often became overwhelming, driving them to utter despair. As hairs were split over the proper wording of a phrase, a loneliness could have set in at times, perhaps causing one to consider ridding oneself once and for all of the "hideous task" that hovered above, threatening to suffocate the "small, insignificant individual" who dared to encroach upon this "forbidden, impossible territory."

But they toiled on, driven by a pioneer spirit, a self-inflicted natural curiosity, a determination unmatched by most humans. Rather than merely have an unorganized set of opinions, they felt it necessary to inspect, scrutinize, and organize these concepts into a meaningful and coherent system of views. And by tackling and becoming enmeshed within these problems, each felt he could achieve a more significant comprehension and appreciation of this world.

PART THREE
INTERVIEW WITH AN ALERT AMERICAN

Plato scratched an itchy part of his nose. He was riding a bus enroute to Portsmouth, intently watching people driving past in cars or striding by foot at the roadside.

He had a special admiration for the inhabitants of the United States, highly impressed by their ingenuity and rugged individualism, as he had observed history unfold from way up above earth. He felt somewhat close to Americans, having paid extra attention to them for a long time now. Among the Great Thinkers, Plato was currently regarded as the foremost expert on the United States.

Plato argued vehemently and was instrumental in persuading the other philosophers to embark to the States. Many of them were at first reluctant, deriding Plato as being "overly presumptuous." They said, "What do you think, you can just drop in and be heralded as a totally believable sage, filled with words of wisdom that people will actually embrace?"

But the others also felt an endearing, although cautious, attraction to the Americans, recognizing that these people, with their basic ideas of freedom, had a special role to play, one that could benefit the world. And, in time, the rest of the philosophers, too, came to realize the need to touch base with the Americans.

Plato gazed out the bus window. Donning his headphones, he began listening to an old-fashioned radio-cassette player. Before he turned up the volume, he thought he heard something mumbled by a curmudgeon seated to the rear, grumbling to the lady at his side that, "In my days, we didn't have those stupid headphones. Bad for your ears, I tell you. Just downright annoying!" Plato chuckled and switched back and forth between alternative and pop radio stations as the bus pushed along on the final leg of the trip.

After a while, he removed the headphones.

"Where are you going?" asked a middle-aged black woman from across the aisle.

"To Portsmouth," he answered.

"I've been there once, when I was a kid—and a lot slimmer. It's a nice place," she said, drawling out her words.

"Where are you going?" asked Plato.

"I'll get off in Massachusetts. I'm gonna' go fishin'! That's what I'm gonna' do. Worked enough this week. I clean houses. Now, I'm gonna' go fishin'!" she triumphantly asserted, a large grin adorning her face.

Plato smiled. He was a great listener. She told him how she moved up to New England from Mississippi, that she had lived on a farm, and that she once loved a man named Snake.

In time, the bus stopped to let her off. Plato waved goodbye to his friend as yet again she declared, as if on top of the world, "I'm goin' fishin'! That's what I'm gonna' do!"

Two bus riders began sneezing simultaneously. After about a half-dozen highly audible expirations of forced breath attracting significant attention, one of them laughed embarrassingly as she almost apologetically exclaimed to the adjacent passengers, "My allergies are pretty bad this week!" The other sneezer looked quite miserable as he desperately clutched a wet Kleenex.

Plato glanced at his hand-scribbled notes as the bus staggered through a sharp turn and ride participants were pulled from their perpendicular positions, tipped askew of their comfort zones.

The elderly curmudgeon complained, "For crying out loud, can't this driver take it easy around the turns?"

The other Great Minds began arriving on earth no earlier than a week before their symposium, but Plato had worked out a deal to touch down long before that—one month before the presentation. During that time, Plato had traveled slowly by bus and train across the United States. He spoke with many people, but five days ago met an individual who stood out among all the rest. As Plato waited in line to order at a McDonald's, there was a commotion at the cash register where an unkempt burly man was giving a hard time to the cashier as he boisterously insisted he did not want onions and lettuce on his burger. A woman in front of Plato turned around to look at Plato, rolling her eyes and snickering. Holding her delicate hand up to her mouth, she whispered to Plato, directing her wish at the agitated guy at the counter, "Geez, just take the veggies out yourself!" Plato laughed, and they struck up a conversation.

Plato discovered she was a physician who worked at a family clinic. He got a sense that she thoroughly enjoyed her occupation. "Every day, we see many patients," she stated. "All kinds of people, each a real gem. The days go by quickly because we're so busy. It's a great responsibility and honor to be able to care for so many people," she said with a smile.

Plato told her where he was heading and what his purpose was. After a while, he came to see that this young woman had a handle on the raison d'etre of the philosophers' coming. She was a rare voice in the wilderness, thought Plato. "Obviously, I follow the local and national news each day, and read a lot," she responded when asked how she stayed abreast of current events. She said, "Obviously, I am guilty of being part of the relentless pursuit of the perfect life, too; just like everybody else, I guess, although each person handles it differently." He was so intrigued, that he asked her for permission to record an interview with her, to which she enthusiastically agreed. "This recording will help me later as I continue to organize my thoughts," he told her, grasping his chin with his hand.

Plato asked various questions to which she responded in a confident and soft-spoken manner. She talked with passion and clarity, between bites of her cheeseburger and sips of root beer. She had a sense of urgency, getting in as much material as possible within the compressed time available for their conversation.

After Plato finished recording, he warmly thanked the young woman as she picked up her belongings from the McDonald's table and explained that she had to be on her way, traveling to visit her parents. With a smile, she raised her hand and waved as she exited around the corner.

Now, as Plato sat alone on the bus, a few days having transpired since he talked to the petite woman with straight dark hair, he decided he would listen to this recording. He figured he had enough time for the whole cassette tape before arriving in Portsmouth.

Excerpts from the interview:

Q: And so you say—and I agree with you—there is this relentless pursuit of the perfect life. And you mentioned, without going into details, what you called manifestations of this. One of these manifestations is "aloofness." What do you mean by aloofness?

A: About this aloofness: it is growing, is difficult to discern at times, is very subtle. Many would deny its existence. It is a distance that is set up between people in the society as they gradually lose sight of a team mission, camaraderie, and even reality. It is an emphasis upon self, concomitant with an increased isolation.

Q: What is team mission?

A: A team mission means a purpose, a common goal, an objective everyone in the society works toward. When we arise in the morning, do we feel a sense of unity with all other Americans?

A sense of common purpose—that what I plan to do in the upcoming day is going to mesh in some way with everyone else's plans, to collectively produce a positive achievement? Do you wish you had a sense of higher purpose, giving you some meaningful link with other people?

Q: But would everyone agree that a team mission is necessary? Is it even appropriate? It sounds regimental, restrictive of freedom.

A: Many would argue against having a team mission. They would say, "We aren't sheep following blindly. Let individuals be individuals." Well, yes, of course, freedom and individualism must, and can, be preserved in the presence of a team mission. The mission statement is only a general guideline, under which individuals can still be themselves. Having a mission does not mean everyone is to wear identical clothes, act the same, and follow blindly like a fascist leader's automatons. You don't need something like communist propaganda posters pasted up all over the walls to keep a team mission foremost in the national consciousness. It is natural for people to move in independent, uncoordinated directions, as they fulfill their needs, and this is good and desired. However, by inserting a mission, a bit more of the self-serving energy can be directed toward the goal of achieving a collective mission that benefits everyone, and therefore societal progress is increased. So I believe we can argue that a team mission is appropriate and not harmful to the cause of individual freedom.

Is it necessary? In a smoothly-operating organization or winning sports team, chances are there will be a unified goal, a universal purpose. It has been recognized within the business community that having a mission statement is essential for success. A perfect example is Total Quality Management—or whatever the latest buzzword is—calling for a mission statement to be drawn up and returned to for guidance. So, if you want efficiency and progress, having a team mission can't hurt.

Q: Can you give examples of mission statements?

A: A hospital may have a mission worded as follows: "Our mission is to provide medical services in the most caring and effective manner to people of all ages in order to correct or manage disabilities that hinder them from sustaining healthy lifestyles." Whenever a problem or decision point is encountered during day-to-day routine operations, this statement is returned to for guidance. The mission at Pedro's Magazine Shop could be "To continually strive to serve our customers in the most efficient and friendly way possible." Whatever enterprise you find yourself entwined within, when situations grow hectic or chaotic, it is reassuring to return to your mission as you ask, "Just what am I doing here?" It is a way to stay focused.

If a poll is taken asking Americans what their national mission is, there would be an immense diversity of answers. There would be confusion over any universal goals. What is the American people's mission? What goals are we working toward achieving together? To "lead the free world?" To amass as many luxuries as possible? To manufacture better goods than anyone else? To further develop and refine democracy? To make as much money as possible?

In fairness, perhaps all Americans, regardless of their differences, do have a common mission. But whatever it is, it is not articulated clearly and consistently.

Nevertheless, even without an annunciation of a mission, society continues to progress, but imagine how much further it could go if there was a definite higher unifying purpose guiding and influencing people as they move through their daily routines. I'm just talking about a stronger and higher purpose in life than what exists now!

Q: What of the camaraderie?

A: If the mission is the group's purpose, camaraderie is the spirit of the actions taken by the individuals of the group to achieve the purpose. It is team spirit. It is teamwork, as people help each other out. It is a sense of feeling useful, having a deep connection with everybody else. As each person pitches in in his own way, this atmosphere of teamwork pervades the group as it moves toward achieving its goals. Think of the can-do attitudes of the volunteers for a marathon race benefiting cancer research—everyone contributes above and beyond to the overall cause.

Indeed, there is an abundance of camaraderie today, in the form of volunteerism as so many people donate their time to assist sport, scout, 4H, church, and other organizations. A sense of camaraderie takes the form of the multitudes of charitable financial donations given to support good causes. There are plenty of stories of good turns, of Good Samaritans helping someone in need. People pitch in during times of adversity, such as war or natural disasters.

Even so, there still seems to be something missing. The spirit of camaraderie is not consistent or as profound as it could be. It may be high in wartime, but the enthusiasm abruptly wanes soon afterwards. When a hurricane destroys a town, sometimes people help each other rebuild, but sometimes we loot and vandalize or charge exorbitant prices for goods and services while the "economic opportunity" exists. Wouldn't it be nice if that spirit of cooperation that infused those marathon race volunteers continued after the event was finished, when everyone returns to the daily grind? I guess you could say we lack a deeper, more sustained level of genuine camaraderie.

If this camaraderie were present, when you were at work you would care more about the quality you produce not because you were afraid of getting fired, but because you were sincerely concerned about how your work would affect other people. You would know your actions have effects on the entire society's progress. If you did not feel this responsibility, you might fall into the habit of producing sloppy work, rushing through it without paying attention to details just to get home quicker so you could pursue your own personal agenda.

If there was a higher sense of camaraderie, you would strive hard to keep yourself in top physical condition not just for your own benefit but to be an asset to the rest of the world. By being healthy, you accomplish your own tasks more efficiently, which in turn benefits other people. If a building catches fire and a person is injured to the point where self-evacuation is not possible, it would be to that person's advantage if you were strong and healthy enough to carry that person out rather than be unable to accomplish that rescue due to your own poor health. Again, I'm just talking about a higher, sustained level of camaraderie than what already exists now. Imagine the possibilities.

Q: What do you mean when you say there is a distance set up between people as they lose sight of reality?

A: I don't know where you are going in Portsmouth, but a few years ago I came across a seemingly forgotten dilapidated billboard somewhere along the roadside there—I don't know if it's still there; probably not. It had an abandoned advertising message rendered illegible due to its peeled paint and collage of melded graffiti. One graffiti message, however, did stand out in large, bold print:

THE WORLD IS AROUND YOU, BUT YOU ARE IN YOUR CAR

I remember thinking how detached, how aloof we can become from reality when glass is placed between us. When I am in a car, windows closed, people and things outside appear distant—don't seem as real. If you at least rolled down the window in your car while traveling in a snowfall, you would immediately feel a closer connection with what was going on around you. Roll it back up and you lose that. At another time of the year, let's say summer, if you were outside the car, perhaps on a bicycle, you would be encompassed by the wind and sunlight, would smell the flowers and plants, and would feel flies hit your skin. The world, with its wind and rain, ice and cold, is firmly in place outside.

The world is out there! But you are in the car, or in your plush, comfortable living room, for that matter. Sheltered and secure, snuggled warmly on the sofa, here is a sanitary existence far removed from the dirt and sweat found in real life. As we hunker down in the comfort of our own homes, we distance ourselves even further from the realities of the world outside. We fail to catch that there is a relentless pursuit of the perfect life enveloping us.

In that living room, the television often becomes the predominant view to the outside. And when we have had enough viewing, we could easily shut off the television. You could maintain a distance, remain aloof, from what really was going on around you. You did not have to get your hands dirty or feel sweat drip down your forehead. You could watch people suffering on your TV set and feel compassion and cry aloud, "Why don't we do something about this!" Then you could settle back into your soft recliner, calming down a bit, as you take comfort in realizing that your government or someone else must be working on the problem. And you, in your living room, never have to go out and personally meet face-to-face with the real people you want to see helped. You don't have to talk directly to them, don't have to suffer with them. Obviously, it is beneficial to delegate some tasks to the bureaucracy, but the more that gets delegated, the more aloof we become. There is a greater distance between people.

The more comfortable we become in the car and living room, the more comforts we want. It's certainly good to want to be comfortable, but there are dangers if we overdo it. Things start to get ludicrous. Try to fend off your disgruntled passengers if you fail to park your car right next to a store entrance, as they complain about having to walk too far across the parking lot. If you are a teacher grading a test, do not even consider using red ink to mark a student's error since that would only devastate that child's self-esteem and create an uncomfortable situation, even though he'll be ruthlessly graded with incessant red ink as an adult. In this extreme-comfort society, there is an aloofness from reality that distorts our decisions and actions.

As we become more comfortable and distant from reality, the more we take for granted. We expect the electricity to keep working, and lash out when it shuts down. If our airline flight gets delayed because of bad weather, we become appalled that such an inconvenience is being thrown at us. And how many people appreciated what work went into the producing of a can of beef stew? Somebody had to raise the cow. Someone had to plant and harvest the crops. Someone slaughtered the cow. Someone prepared the ingredients for packing into the cans. Someone mined the metal for the can. Someone got the cans into the store. But after living in a sanitary existence for a while, one easily becomes ignorant of or unfeeling toward many of life's realities, taking too much for granted. To get from point A to point B takes effort, an effort too easily forgotten as we snap our fingers and expect all to be sound. When we think and act unreasonably, and overly complain about air flight delays, we distance ourselves further from other people.

And when we do leave the comforts of our living room to enter the increasingly unfamiliar world outside, there is a recklessness that follows. When we, for example, engage in nation-building in some foreign land, we usually do not have a realistic and sufficient understanding of that area of the world. We have been too sheltered and apathetic to really know. When we then proceed to entangle ourselves there, it is like the well-intentioned, though misguided, upper-middleclass family stepping into the ghetto to attempt to amend the way people have been living for generations, aiming to bring them in line with a radically different lifestyle that isn't necessarily better.

So there is a distance between individuals as we lose touch with reality. Driving in a car, you think to yourself: *Get out of my way! Have to be somewhere a few miles from here, and I'm running late.*

Let me pass this guy off—going too slow for me! Swerve into the opposite lane of head-on approaching cars, attempting to pass. That's it ... back into the right lane ... Oh; I think I ran the slow guy off the road. Must've cut him off too tightly. Looks like he may have slammed into boulders at the roadside. That's what it looks like in the rearview mirror. Nah, it probably didn't happen ... or did it? Well, no matter, that's far behind me now. I'll just keep driving ... don't want to be late.

Q: You said another manifestation of the relentless pursuit of the perfect life was the development of a disposable society. What is this?

A: America has become a "disposable society." If something is in the way of your perfect life, just dispose of it, get rid of the annoyance. There is an easy disposability of people or principles if these should obstruct the path to the perfect life. If you tire of a marriage, just get a divorce. Don't let the spouse be an obstacle to your perfect life. If your parents are too old and slow, this may impede your life's progress, so put them in a nursing home. If you are carrying something you need to throw away but there is no garbage can within an arm's length distance, just discard the trash on the sidewalk or side of the road. When the kids are annoying, send them to watch TV, or hire a nanny. Don't let anyone obstruct your path to the perfect life. Continue what you must to enjoy yourself. There are movies to watch, cocktail hours to attend. You have to work hard to amass enough money to purchase the hot tub. Material luxuries abound—don't miss the opportunities. Most of us now live above what is called the subsistence level; that is, our basic needs in life are taken care of and we have money and time left over to spend on other wants. This was not the case two-hundred years ago when every waking minute had to be invested in the arduous work of survival. Nowadays we have more time to devote to the much deserved pursuit of the increasingly available luxuries, but this pursuit has a dangerous tendency to often become selfishly relentless, at the expense of other people. We live "fast" lives, where there is no time for children because they would only impede us as we continue our pursuit of the perfect life we feel we are owed. There is too much money to earn and so little time to play. And so the kids get neglected. In a sense, they are discarded. And these things occur in subtle ways that slowly envelop us more and more. As the well-intentioned social engineer spends countless hours writing laws that are to better the lives of the general public he cares deeply about, the family lives close around him may be suffering with neglect.

Q: And there is a disposal of principles?

A: We lack moral consistency. Many of us accept one set of principles one day, only to discard those the next, adopting instead another violently contrasting set of principles in order to satisfy individual desires or needs of that particular moment. This becomes a habitual practice, giving rise to behavior patterns of moral inconsistency with the intent of maximizing personal convenience. A person easily throws away any firm convictions he or she may have held high one moment, in order to make an extra dollar profit or obtain an additional moment of pleasure. Headlines are filled with stories of dishonesty: the illegal stock market trading, the hypocrisy of TV ministers, broken promises of politicians. This is only the iceberg's tip, for below the surface, manifesting on local levels, involving families and small towns, is a plethora of dishonesty, of moral inconsistency.

Q: Can you give examples of that?

A: One man may assert on Tuesday that he definitely does not believe abortion is moral and that he would never coerce someone to get one. On Wednesday, his girlfriend announces she is pregnant and he is responsible along with her. On Thursday, he realizes the personal burden he will inherit. On Friday, he provides money for the abortion and urges his girlfriend to get it done as soon as possible. On the day a hunter obtains his license, he also pledges to uphold the hunting laws of his society. The next day he kills an animal intentionally even though it is illegal to do so at that particular time of year. If asked why he did this, he may state confidently, perhaps triumphantly, that it was OK to do this only because he was pretty certain he was not going to "get caught." The fact that he was not going to get caught was enough to make his act legal, in his own way of thinking. To him, the pledge just did not hold much weight, even though it and the hunting laws were carefully developed to serve a serious, important purpose. One day, the president of a chemical company affirms publicly that he will always abide by legal waste-dumping guidelines. The next day, he authorizes his employees to dump toxic wastes at sites and in ways that are not officially approved as safe, legal, and acceptable. He allows this to occur only because this is cheaper and more profitable. He knows it is not legal, knows that human and environmental damage will occur, and knows that if done secretly and with extreme caution he will escape detection by the authorities. In today's world, we walk around and get hit from all sides by such a large diversity of ideas—which is good—but it is not good when people have a deficiency of well thought-out, firm guiding principles that serve as a baseline from which all these radically different ideas can be distilled. There is a pattern of inconsistency in our daily actions that results. One concept may be adopted even though it is inconsistent with another concept that a person may hold dear. So, ours is a disposable society; we simply discard a principle, a person, or an object if it interferes with our quest for the perfect life.

Q: How does this inconsistency with principles affect progress?

A: When a person takes rolls of toilet papers or bars of soap from public facilities in order to stock his own home, he contributes in a small but significant way to the raising of that facility's prices; the owner must compensate for loss due to theft. If less people stole from stores, prices would go down. A far-fetched example, yes, but in its own way an illustration of a seemingly insignificant problem that, when added to others, creates a collectively powerful force that burdens progress. In a technical school where students must complete a certain amount of projects in a given amount of time, the quantity of projects may be unrealistically excessive, but because the majority of students cheat, they accomplish the tasks. This sends a message to the school administrators that the requirement is not excessive, since the vast majority of students pass the tests, but the honest student who attempts to complete the projects on his own without cheating may be the unfortunate person who fails the requirement and has to suffer the consequences. If the majority did not cheat, a more accurate analysis of the required projects and allotted time could be had by the administrators, and more realistic requirements could be set. We may often find a person who is a member of a business corporation, attempting to climb the ladder of promotions, mislead superiors in a report of certain activities he or she directed. The deception was done in order to protect that person's reputation in the eyes of superiors so that advancement in rank would not be jeopardized. The activity directed by that person may have fallen short of productivity quotas or there may have been errors that would signal poor management of the project, so the final report is "fudged" to appear more favorable. This in effect sends wrong ideas to the superiors that will just invite future miscalculations rather than accurate readjustments of existing policy.

When we mislead, we deny other people the ability to make good choices, since the truth is not present to guide them in their decisions. When a decision based on deception is enacted, the adverse consequences eventually disseminate to other people, everyone losing something. And when we do not follow rules, the same happens—the progress of society is hindered.

*

As Plato traveled through the States, he read newspapers in which it was commonplace to find headlines saying that Florida tourists were murdered by teenagers for no apparent motive other than it having been a fun thing to do and that two small children were left home alone by their vacationing parents and that there was an increased suicide rate among children and that the number of single parents was multiplying rapidly and that a child sued to permanently disown his parents and that schools needed to invest much money into security to try to hinder the bringing of guns into the classrooms and that memberships to violent youth gangs were on the upswing and that youngsters were increasingly involved with carjackings and that a "wilding" spree in a park ended in a brutal rape of a young woman by a band of kids "who had nothing better to do" and that jail terms have become a rite of passage and were highly desired by some teens wishing to gain stature among peers and that a five-year-old boy and a seven-year-old boy were caught knocking over tombstones at a cemetery and that teenagers destroyed a house during a party but felt no remorse whatsoever and that a parent pummeled an infant to death because the baby would not stop crying and wet her diaper too often and that a sixteen-year-old killed a fifty-nine-year-old because "the old man pulled away from the stop sign too slowly" and that the high school dropout rate exceeded twenty-five percent in certain locales and that a young mother strapped her two small children to their car seats in the backseat and then pushed the car into a lake, watching the babies struggle as they gradually submerged into the water.

*

Q: Yes? You want to add something more?

A: About the disposal of principles—dishonesty is rife. One might say, "Well, that's just a little white lie, a white-collar crime—it's not morally bad," but the prevalence and relative acceptability of the "little" crimes make it that much easier for the big crimes, that is, the violent ones, to occur. Each time a community is traumatized by a violent crime, our progress toward a better society is hampered. We all experience a setback in some way, even if we do not immediately feel it.

Q: You said another manifestation of the relentless pursuit of the perfect life is a pervasive victimization. What is "victimization?"

A: There is a growing tendency to victimization, which is when you exaggeratingly claim yourself to be abused or persecuted, subjected to oppression, hardship, or mistreatment. You then proceed to claim you are owed compensation for the wrong inflicted on you. You tend to find no fault with your own shortcomings while you blame only others when things do not go your own way. You might establish a formal complaint, or cite blame during routine dialogue, or file a self-indulgent lawsuit, or just claim various entitlements from the government. When an "inconvenience" is presented to our nice, sanitary and perfect lives, we cry "foul" or use it as an excuse. One could find parents blaming doctors, and suing them, if their new baby is a girl and not a boy as they had hoped. It is even imaginable that one day one of us may try to sue the President for an earthquake that ruins a backyard swimming pool.

Q: It is understood that the number of lawsuits is at a phenomenal level. Is this what you see?

A: Of course. Some guy was given the wrong prescription drug and it colored his urine blue. He alerted his physician, who quickly corrected the situation by prescribing a different drug. The patient did not suffer any adverse physiological effects and was well on the way to full recovery from his ailment, but he sued the doctor because the blue urine "caused him extreme embarrassment" while he urinated in public restrooms that day. The patient subsequently won the lawsuit and was awarded a large sum of money. A "Dear Ann Landers" letter told of a person who was suing a department store for not having a diaper-changing table in the men's room. A jail prisoner was suing because his rice pudding did not have raisins. A lady sued because the coffee she purchased at McDonald's was too hot and burned her when she spilled it on herself while sitting in her car. A boy slipped on a public playground swing. He suffered a few bruises which subsequently healed. His father sued the city because he said "the playground equipment is obviously unsafe." The city's taxes had to be raised so revenue could be gained to pay for the ensuing legal battles.

Do not misunderstand me. It is good we have the legal system. It is a necessary institution serving a protective role that contributes to progress, and many lawsuits are legitimate, but in the current state of affairs, the legal system is often abused, thereby detracting from progress. It is apparent that many persons, in their claims of victim status, have legitimate gripes. However, the problem is that victim status is being abused, carried to an extreme. It is difficult to know who is sincere and who is playing a deception.

Q: And you may blame anyone or anything other than yourself?

A: If an ice hockey coach beats up a referee because of a disagreement over a ruling in a tough game, it is popular now to blame this action on an unhappy childhood or on the influence of television, or you may hear the "I was just having a bad day" explanation. If an individual cannot hold a job, keeps getting fired, he could blame this on prejudice of employers toward, perhaps, his heavy weight or his minority status, or other condition. Never mind that he may have been negligent in his duties while on the job. There must be someone or something else to blame. If your child fails to win an art contest, you may claim her to be a victim of unfair bias. If you are caught driving under the influence of alcohol, blame the bar owners for serving you too much. One guy blamed his action of murdering another person on the fact that he ate too many Twinkies that day.

There is a feeling that one has a right to do whatever he or she wants, forgetting that concomitant with rights are responsibilities. There was an individual who burned down a forest, claiming freedom of expression. Jesse Burnham[1]*, in *Time* magazine, wrote that "This is the age of the self-tort crybaby, to whom some disappointment—a slur, the loss of a job, an errant spouse, a foul-tasting can of beer, a slip on the supermarket floor, an unbecoming face-lift—is sufficient occasion to claim huge monetary awards." Burnham also stated in the article that "Public affairs professor William Galston of the University of Maryland says the practice of blaming others stems from unrealistic expectations of the modern, risk-avoiding age. "If something bad happens to us," he says, "we are outraged because our lives are supposed to be perfect."

Q: And what about entitlements?

A: We are demanding more entitlements from government: medical care, retirement benefits, unemployment pay, disability pay, childcare, and so on. It is as if we feel we are victims of an unjust society and so are owed compensation. If we failed to purchase flood insurance while we owned property in an obvious flood zone, and a flood occurs, we have come to expect the government to cover the expenses. The government increasingly takes up the role of being parent to children as it encroaches upon territory formerly reserved exclusively for parents; for example,

---

1 actually, *Jesse Birnbaum* wrote this in the August 1991 edition of *Time* magazine; the woman simply mispronounced the last name.

people have gradually authorized healthcare providers to enter the public schools and perform dental services on the students. You could debate the merits of this—there's certainly much good that can come of it—but getting children to the doctor was traditionally a responsibility given to parents and many experts feel this new development actually impedes real progress. They say government is not as effective in carrying out these basic tasks and, more importantly, items are being taken away from the parent checklist of things-to-do. The more entitlements people receive, the less responsibility they have to deal with. This makes them a bit more aloof.

Q: And finally, what is the decline in health all about? This is the last manifestation that you mentioned.

A: There is a decline in physical, as well as mental, health. Alexander Solzhenitsyn remarked, referring to the Western world, that "Every citizen has been granted the desired freedom and material goods in such quantity and of such quality as to guarantee in theory the achievement of happiness. In the process, however, one psychological detail has been overlooked: the constant desire to have still more things and a still better life, and the struggle to obtain them, imprints many Western faces with worry and even depression, though it is customary to conceal such feelings." We have increased incidences of mental depression because we feel the strains of trying to keep up with the neighbors in the pursuit of our wants. People put extensive pressure on themselves as they try to keep up with that Jones family or else begin to feel inadequate. The stress drives a trend of spending beyond one's means so there is an overuse of credit cards, for example, with large, unmanageable debts accruing. I've also seen young newlyweds leap immediately into huge houses and have to face the burden of working so hard to pay for this that they really don't find quality time to actually enjoy living there. This is so different from my situation in which I lived in small apartments for years with my spouse before we could comfortably afford to move into a more spacious home. We didn't approach it as, "I want it, and I want it now!" Sure, I make a lot of mistakes just like the next person, of course, but with the housing issue, I think I got it right.

Obesity is on the increase among adults and children. There is a diminished self-restraint when it comes to eating and drinking, while simultaneously less engagement in physical activity. Someone recently told me you could easily spot American tourists in other countries because they would be "the heaviest ones rolling about." I shouldn't say that! They're not all large. But, anyway, the point is that the decline of health detracts from progress in many ways that should be apparent.

Q: Do you think you go overboard in criticizing your neighbors? That you might be a bit unfair regarding your characterization of Americans?

A: Don't misunderstand me (laughter) … there is so much good out there, and I certainly hope for the best, but I'm not blind, either.

PART FOUR
NEW ACQUAINTANCES DOWNTOWN

The bus's engine began winding down as the vehicle was about to terminate its conveyance of the passengers to their destination. The bus stopped at Market Square, the heart and center of Portsmouth.

Plato slung his backpack over his shoulder and made his way to the front of the bus. No one knew who he was. He paused to let a woman out of her seat, her two young children following. She smiled at him and he said to her, "Have a nice day!"

Without fanfare, people exited the bus and emerged onto the sidewalk where many people were walking around or sitting on benches. Plato picked up his suitcase and headed toward his hotel, which was a few blocks away. The bell of the North Church tolled to let everyone know it was ten o'clock in the morning.

Plato had the look of a forty-year old, in great health. One of his shoelaces came undone, so he bent down to refasten it. Someone's fuzzy little puppy hopped its way over to him, and he reached out to pet the playful animal. He smiled at its attractive owner as she tugged back on the leash. She smiled back. Then Plato continued on his way.

Granite steps in the area of the bus-stop led pedestrians to partially sheltered benches. The sidewalks were of red brick, with small trees planted to grow through the masonry at various sites, adorning the urban atmosphere as they stretched skyward.

Colorful flowers decorated the downtown. Many people were outdoors on this Saturday, enjoying the beautiful day.

A group of young people hung out on the street corner in front of the church. Whatever they were talking about seemed serious, as a couple of them stressed points with sharp hand gestures. Some of them appeared angry.

Melody Wynn owned and operated a jewelry store. She had a habit of often ceasing abruptly in mid-sentence to belt out some smidgen of a song that would serve to further develop the conversation's message, returning to the spoken word thereafter to complete the sentence. The "Singing Lady," as she was called, could sometimes aggravate people with her musical acrobatics, but mostly her skilled voice swiftly redeemed her. When Plato walked by, she talked-sang to a young couple she knew well something about "I told you—sooner or later, love is gonna' get yuh!"

Plato laughed when he saw a bunch of preschoolers shaking hands with someone dressed as Barney the Dinosaur. Plato strode over to him or her and said, "Hi, Barney," as he shook the purple paw.

The wide variety of shops had their windows decorated with eye-catching displays. There were stores for women's dresses, for shoes, for imported crafts. There were restaurants with many ethnic cuisines represented—Japanese, Chinese, Thai, Mexican, Irish, Italian, Indian, as well as American. A tattoo parlor beckoned passersby to come in for a durable souvenir. Videos could be rented, kitchen utensils bought, and packages mailed to distant shores. The smell of freshly-baked bread commanded the vicinity of a corner bakery. The import store looked like a museum filled with strange goods that originated from distant jungles and alleyways throughout the world.

Some pedestrians were window-browsing. Others were in town to zoom in on one particular store, make a fast purchase, and then get out as fast as they arrived. Still others, like Bob and Carl, were just there to check out the people and their activities.

For a few minutes, Plato sat on a granite wall that encompassed a colorful floral display, at the corner of the main thoroughfare. He gazed upward at the tall-spired church directly across the street. He then turned his eyes to watch the cars drive slowly past, stopping for pedestrians at the crosswalks. A symbol was painted on the pavement before each crossing lane, instructing motorists to yield. Plato was amused to see the different styles of street-crossing exhibited by the pedestrians. Some would halt abruptly as soon as their feet arrived at the junction of the sidewalk and crosswalk, waiting patiently for permission to proceed from the involved automobile drivers. Others did not even look to see if a car was coming, but just kept walking with an air of confidence that any cars would appropriately halt. Some individuals were inclined, as they strode across the walkway, to hail the cars with a friendly, happy, "Thank you," while others did not gesture at all.

The tobacco shop owner came out into the fresh air of the sidewalk and bought a hot dog from the deeply-tanned and weathered food vendor. The music store cashier escaped from her register for a moment to stretch out her arms toward the sky, as she yelled a greeting to her old friend across the street. The candle shop shelf-stocker came outside to borrow a match from the parking meter reader, so she could smoke a cigarette on her break.

Guitar Jake strummed gentle ballads over by the blue mailbox, and a small, grateful crowd gathered. His voice was tender this day, unlike last week's raspiness after he had spent an evening at one of the local clubs, shouting political ideas during a discussion with a friend, while some loud band's dissonant background chords inundated the room's confines. The upcoming presidential election was a hot topic everywhere.

Jack Beane stuck his head outside his coffee shop to check on the sidewalk tables and chairs. They were in a little disarray, but all was clean and people were enjoying themselves, sipping espresso or regular coffee.

A guy talking on a cell phone came around the corner, his very young daughter in tow. He was intensely discussing the fluctuations of the stock market and how he would have to move his assets around. Everyone who was in the vicinity certainly heard everything, loudly and clearly, since he spoke with such a boisterous tone. His daughter tried frantically to ask him a question, but he just motioned to her to keep quiet.

After a while, Plato rose from the wall and began strolling along the sidewalk. He passed the place that made fresh natural fruit and vegetable drinks. He was fascinated by how rapidly the food handlers could grind down a carrot by pushing it into the blender, a bright orange beverage emerging.

Someone elbowed Plato and said, "Hey, Plato! How's it going?"

It was Epictetus, one of the Great Minds. Plato smiled and asked him, "When did you arrive?"

"I got here three days ago. It's been great. And by the way, I'd like you to meet John and Michelle, two wonderful people. They're showing me around."

Plato shook their hands. They talked briefly and then Epictetus said, "We have to hitch a ride to the Fox Run Mall. We'll catch you later!"

Plato waved goodbye and said, "See you later! And it was nice to meet you, John and Michelle!"

Plato continued along the sidewalk. The hotel where he had made reservations emerged into view at the end of a narrow side street. Plato entered and rang the bell at the front desk. A young man appeared from the back room.

"Hello. I'd like to check in. Name is Plato."

"Oh yes, sir." The clerk looked as if he were slightly aware of the importance of the person before him even though he probably did not know what Plato actually declared in his philosophical dialogues centuries ago. Plato thought, it must seem strange to everyone that he was not wearing an ancient Greek robe and sandals.

After the clerk issued the key, Plato entered his room and threw his suitcase on the bed. His hair was trimmed very short, above his ears, and was black with touches of grey. He removed his jeans and donned shorts and a black T-shirt, slung his ever-present backpack over his shoulder and headed for the public library, just a few blocks away.

On the way to the library, Plato entered a hardware store with the express intention of purchasing a set of screwdrivers, as he felt a definite need for a fresh collection, his old set worn and injured from years of use. He had discovered accommodations for the philosophers, nestled high above Earth somewhere in the clouds, to be rather wanting. Dripping faucets, lack of hot water, and power outages were frequent annoyances. Maintenance support was slow, and over time Plato learned through necessity to act as his own home-repairman.

Plato stood by a shelf in the store, examining the tools. This is when thirty-two year old Byron Dink, one of the local townsfolk, met Plato. Byron walked by him, catching sight of the generic luggage tag, still fastened to his backpack. The tag had "Plato" printed in the name section. Byron could not read the address. He was aware the Great Minds were in Portsmouth for the week, but had not yet seen any of them.

Being shy to initiate conversations, at first Byron hesitated, strolling over to a section of the hardware store housing books on how to place ceramic floor tile. Pretending to be interested, he fumbled through some article on the proper usage of cutting tools, then looked up—yes, Plato was still standing there—and tried to shove this book back into its slot on the shelf. In his haste, he dropped the book onto the floor, and, when he stooped down to retrieve it, succeeded in whapping his head on the shelf's edge. Rubbing the sore spot, he sneaked a glance in the direction of Plato and then meekly returned the book back to its home on the shelf.

Fortunately, within a few minutes he managed to muster a little courage. It was a sudden surge of inspiration and curiosity that pushed him. Striding over to Plato, he politely said, "Excuse me, are you one of the visiting philosophers? I couldn't help but notice your luggage tag … ?"

Plato smiled and said, "I'm Plato. Yes, I'm one of them. Just visiting briefly. And you … you are … ?"

"Byron … Byron Dink." Shaking hands and looking into Plato's supposedly ancient eyes, which actually seemed to Byron no different than any ordinary person's eyes, he exclaimed, "This is so amazing! It is an honor to meet you!"

But in the next instant, Byron's guard went up and the amazement turned more cautious. "So what is this anyway? Some kind of joke? Or corporate promotion? What's the deal?" Byron fidgeted with his glasses, which had slid down his steeply-sloped nose.

"No, this is real," Plato replied, well aware that people would be skeptical.

Plato changed the subject, explaining that he "was just looking for a suitable set of screwdrivers and I think I've found the one I need here. So you know that today we will be presenting some ideas in a symposium open to the public, at the Sheraton?"

Byron had read about the event in the newspaper. As he rubbed his prematurely balding head, he tried to remember the teachings of Plato so that he might speak somewhat intelligently to this person whom he felt was just impersonating the ancient Greek. A few years back, he'd studied Plato's writings in college, but could not focus now on the details. *There was something about a Blank Slate … but what else? Maybe it will start coming back to me ….*

"This city is very beautiful. Do you live here?" Plato inquired.

"Yes. I live in an apartment. Near here."

"Well, I certainly am glad we chose this city for our guest appearance. It looks like it will make for a wonderful time. Are you busy? Can you go outside with me after I purchase this?"

Byron nodded. "Would you like to see more of this town?"

"Yes, that would be great! My intention was to get to the library, but I'll go later," Plato answered.

They walked to Market Square, watching the people of all shapes and demeanors flitting about. The city was lively. As they came upon a toy store, Plato peered through the window to see kid's sticker books featuring philosophers. There was a short biography for each historic figure, with a place to affix a corresponding full-color portrait stamp. The books were on sale to commemorate the festive activities surrounding the Great Minds.

They continued walking. "Byron, here's someone I know," Plato said, pointing, as he hailed Karl Marx, another of the Great Minds. Marx, his long hair oscillating in the breeze, held up a shopping bag so Plato could see he had something inside that he wanted to show him.

"Check this out, Plato!" he said, unveiling a small plastic statue of Rodin's *The Thinker* from its paper wrapping. "Capitalism at its best. These were specially made for today's events. I figured I'd buy a couple to take back as souvenirs, regardless of how kitschy they are."

Plato laughed and then introduced him to Byron. Then Marx continued on his way, having spotted more souvenirs on sale at another store.

The guy with the cell phone walked by again and, once more, his daughter was trying to get his attention. He was busy, however, discussing last night's baseball games, the phone held tightly against his ear. He apparently had no idea his daughter, meanwhile, was busy too, lifting merchandise from the sidewalk shelves and putting it all into a shopping bag. It looked like she had quite a few items innocently stashed away. Plato chuckled.

Byron tried to figure out the real story behind this "philosopher promotion." He was in an adventurous mood and decided to go along with what he called the "charade." Anyway, it probably would all be explained in tomorrow's newspaper, he surmised.

Byron took note of Plato's calm demeanor. Plato never raised his voice and he seemed to be in complete control at all times, unafraid to confront any question or idea that came his way. There was a certain air of dignity about the way he carried himself.

"Tell me a little about you, Byron," Plato requested.

Byron sat on the stone window sill outside a newspaper shop. "I was born here and have lived here all my life. After I graduated from the University of New Hampshire, I got a job at an insurance company and have been there ever since. My girlfriend is Angela. She's out of town this weekend."

They discussed the relentless pursuit of the perfect life. Plato played excerpts from the cassette interview. Byron listened intently, figuring he would maybe learn something from this stranger, who seemed amicable enough. Byron had an ability to let others first have their full say before he would render final judgments or opinions. He had been a college student with a slight interest in philosophy, although time allotted for this study was limited by his regular curriculum, work, and social activities.

Responding to his discussions with Plato and the taped interview, Byron said, "Yeah, I think you're on to something there. I never thought about it this much, but have seen those things—those manifestations—from time to time."

Byron, however, felt that Plato was exaggerating the degree to which he claimed this "relentless pursuit of the perfect life" had evolved to harm the society. But he tried to keep an open mind and later admitted that perhaps there was some veracity to the story.

Byron recommended the horse-drawn carriage ride, and Plato accepted the invitation. The carriage would convey them to one of the historic districts, Strawberry Banke, and back. A bearded driver directed them aboard, then motioned to the horses to begin trotting alongside the cars.

Traffic was light. The sun was warm and nicely complimented the slightly cool breeze that periodically stirred the air.

"Now, I don't know if I understand this completely. That is, what *do* you do? I mean, for all those centuries?" Byron ventured.

"It's a long story," Plato laughed. "Let's just say I've seen a great many things."

Plato often held his chin with his right hand, as if pondering, deep in thought.

"So this is really fascinating. I can't believe I'm riding in the twenty-first century A.D. with someone from B.C.!"

"Stranger things, perhaps, can happen."

"Of course, you could be pulling my leg, making this whole thing up ... " Byron retorted, still not buying this deal.

Plato shook his head, and then smiled.

The equipage driver twisted his torso around so he could face his passengers. He said, "Welcome to our simple form of transportation. Make yourselves comfortable. Enjoy the ride! Beautiful weather we've had, eh?"

They eventually trotted past Town Hall, with its colonial architecture atop a gentle hill overlooking the downtown and a decorous park. A small lake lay below, its still waters reflecting the adjoining buildings and trees like a bright mirror. There were colorful shrubs decorating the landscape. Long, sharp steeples pierced the air, pointing skyward, accenting the horizon. This city was of the sort that would appear just right if placed in miniature under a Christmas tree. There was a dreamy quality encompassing it all.

There were obviously other chance encounters between lucky Portsmouth denizens and Great Minds, like the one between Byron and Plato, during the week. The philosophers were ambassadors with the task of getting a message out, and were available to anyone who was interested.

Plato asked Byron, "Why do you think Americans have become so relentless in their pursuit of a perfect life?"

"I don't know. Maybe … " began Byron, " … maybe it has something to do with giving a man an inch and then he will take two inches?"

"Why does he take two?"

"I don't know. Well, maybe it is allowed, is not challenged, by the person who gave the first inch … " answered Byron.

"Yes, but the extra inch may have been grabbed when the person giving the first inch was not looking, having never intended to give more."

"Yeah, very often that would be the case. I guess people always want more. And they'll do a lot of evil things to get more. But, you know, that hunger is not uniquely American. This kind of thing has happened throughout human history, to all societies, not just American … " Byron defensively exclaimed.

"But the significant difference is the degree to which it has grown in America. Why is that?"

"I guess there are a lot of factors that led to that. I'm not sure … " responded Byron. "Maybe it has something to do with there being an emphasis, in this freedom-loving country, on being all you can be, on going out to get everything you can! And *now*! Everybody wants everything now."

"And at the same time, there is a de-emphasis on self-restraint," Plato added.

One of the horses whinnied and a small boy pointed to it as he giggled. His mother was holding his hand.

"I assume you are a Red Sox fan?" asked Plato.

"Of course. Just about everyone around here is. We finally broke the curse of Babe Ruth. You've heard of that?"

"Oh yes. It had been a while since you won a World Series. Is that correct?"

"That's right," replied Byron. "We came close in 1986, but fell short. We had to wait until the next century to do it, but we eventually prevailed. Two World Series titles so far in this decade."

The carriage rounded a sharp curve in the road as the horses' hooves clunked along on the journey. The streets here were extremely narrow. Everything seemed compressed. The houses were very closely situated together. Yards were tiny. The street lights were reminiscent of the early colonial oil lamps.

"Portsmouth," offered Byron "is the historic site where the Treaty of Portsmouth was negotiated to end the Russo-Japanese War. The local community was heavily involved in moving the diplomatic negotiations forward."

"Yes, I am familiar with this," said Plato. "This war is now known as World War Zero because of the huge armies and navies that engaged and the modern weapons of mass destruction employed."

"That's right. It was a precursor to World War I and II," added Byron.

"Yes," acknowledged Plato, "and the treaty was signed on September 5, 1905."

"Ah, I had forgotten the exact date," responded Byron.

Two beautifully-colored butterflies flitted near the two men as they rode in the carriage. A bluebird flew straight across their path. The sun shone brightly.

They returned to Market Square, where Plato and Byron disembarked and thanked the driver for the tour. A gentle wind blew as they began strolling along the sidewalk again.

At an information kiosk, a volunteer was passing out booklets about the Great Minds. Byron asked Plato, "Did the Great Minds finance those?"

"Yes, we did," answered Plato.

"How did you pay for it?" Byron inquired.

"We pulled off some interesting fundraisers!" Plato said as he chuckled.

The two men were interrupted by a screeching car pulling out from the intersection. As they continued walking, Byron put his sunglasses on.

"I think my bald spot got a mild sunburn," Byron lamented as he lightly touched the top of his head.

They walked to the place where the bus had earlier dropped off Plato. Byron told a short, innocent joke. They laughed. Plato then related a funny, insignificant story, and they laughed again. Then they entered into a serious dialogue as they sauntered toward the library.

PART FIVE
DIALOGUES

Plato: As you might already know, a long time ago, Byron, I wrote books in dialogue form, with many characters appearing——like Socrates, for example. I, however, never presented myself in the drama that unfolded. So I was just thinking—why not try my hand at it now? Is that OK with you?

Byron: Sounds good.

Plato: This way we do not have to get bogged down having to insert parentheses every time somebody talks! And I won't have to add remarks like "Plato said wearily" or "he asked, excitedly."

Byron: Yeah, fine with me.

ON RESTRAINTS

Plato: If people desired to slow down the relentless pursuit of the perfect life, they would need to have external and internal controls, or restraints, which would regulate human behavior.

Byron: I'm not sure I know what you mean.

Plato: External control means behavior regulation of the individual by other individuals. The regulation originates from outside the individual. For example, laws and government regulations are established to direct people's behavior. These are external controls. When driving a car, you must follow laws that say you are to come to a complete stop at stop signs, yield at yield signs, obey the speed limits, signal when you are to make a right or left turn, and get your car inspected once a year. If you own a car repair facility, you must follow certain regulations regarding hazardous waste disposal and regulations concerning workplace safety. If you fail to comply with laws and regulations, you may be punished by, for example, a fine, jail time, public outcry, or a lawsuit, the punishment being another external control. Physical restrictions that prevent people from carrying out certain undesired actions are external controls. For example, tamper-resistant packaging on medicines restricts a person from intentionally contaminating the product so to inflict harm on other people. Automobile anti-theft devices or home security systems are other examples of these external controls.

Byron: When you buy a CD from the music store, the cashier has to unlock it from its anti-theft packaging.

Plato: Indeed. What are other examples of external controls?

Byron: Pay before you pump at gas stations, I guess?

Plato: Yes. The gas station has created its own regulation in order to prevent people from driving off without paying.

Byron: At many public restrooms, a fixed dose of water flows from the faucet after you activate it, then automatically stops. Sometimes you barely get enough water. It is inconvenient, but the facility's management installs this system because too many people would otherwise waste water by allowing too much to run.

Plato: And so they have to resort to external control to regulate how much water is released.

Byron: So external control coerces people to act in a certain way.

Plato: Yes.

Byron: And what would be internal control?

Plato: Internal control is behavior regulation of the individual by the individual himself. There is no fear of punishment from society if he fails to act in the proscribed way. The punishment for failing to act properly comes from within each person—not from without, or externally. You see, the punishment is inflicted by the person upon himself and is the remorse that he feels from letting down others on the team. This remorse is deeply felt because the individual has a pure desire to not only attain his wants for himself but also to allow others to attain theirs too. Internal control is self-regulation. It originates from within the individual.

As they walked past a candy store, Plato interrupted their dialogue when he suddenly stopped, turned around, and motioned to Byron to enter with him. A lady with her hair in a bun greeted them and said, "Welcome to my store. You know this is a sample shop. Just let me know if you'd like to try anything."

Plato nodded to her, and then tapped Byron's shoulder. "Yes! This is what I was looking for!" Plato exclaimed. On the corner of a display case that held multitudes of fine chocolates and other confectionary delights, was an old-fashioned scale for measuring weights.

"This scale represents the controls on the pursuit of wants. One side holds the external controls, while the other the internal," Plato said.

There were a few people in the store, and they all looked over at the two men.

"Allow me to demonstrate to you," continued Plato. "I'll take a handful of these red fishes ... what are they called? Swedish fish? ... and place them on the left side receptacle. This represents the external controls. And next I'll put ten of these truffles in the right, representing the internal controls. The greater weight of the truffles brings the right receptacle down to a lower level than the one holding the flexible fish. This relationship between external and internal represents the ideal position, a more desirable one."

Plato then removed enough truffles so that both sides were at the same horizontal level.

"And even if there was a balance between the two sides, that would not be such a bad position for a society to be in. Unfortunately, the way the weight, in today's society, actually lines up ... " he began to explain but was interrupted by an elderly woman who, gesturing to a large bin of assorted milk chocolates, began pointing excitedly.

"Try these," she declared. "These are very good ... and they should fit just nicely right on that scale! I'm going to buy some today for my three grandchildren."

Plato warmly thanked her, accepting a handful of candy which he placed on the left with the red fishes—the side of the external controls.

Plato then continued, "Unfortunately, this is the reality of the arrangement." The left side lowered with the greater weight as the opposite side lifted higher.

"More weight is placed by society," responded Byron, "on the external."

Plato said, "We tend to place much more faith in the external controls."

"But that should be preferred, anyway. Right? That should be obvious to anyone who is not naïve and foolish," Byron reacted. "The external controls are a sure-shot way to go. If you rely on each person policing himself, you would be gullible. You would be asking for trouble. That would be a dreamer's way to go. We mostly need some kind of external regulation."

The two men, in disagreement, departed the candy store and continued on their way to the library, returning to their dialogues.

Byron: So why, exactly, are the internal controls preferred?

Plato: Because external controls cost money, effort, and freedom. That means less progress.

Byron: How so?

Plato: Because the more you rely on external control, the more money, and the more effort in time and energy you must expend on enforcement of those controls. Time, money, and energy that would be better spent elsewhere.

Byron: The enforcement part of it means more policing, more monitoring of people's activities so violations could be detected.

Plato: And then violations must be dealt with by some form of punishment, which also is another part of enforcement that costs additional time, money, and energy.

Byron: And part of enforcement is also that you have to construct a lot of physical barriers which would make it harder to violate a law in the first place.

Plato: Like those self-regulating faucets. And, as you know, those physical controls cost money. In a store, you have mirrors positioned all over, and you have security personnel monitoring the situation. All of this costs money, the expense ultimately being passed on to you, the consumer. Progress is obstructed.

Byron: And you said external controls cost freedom?

Plato: Freedom, and common sense, too. Every year, more laws and regulations and physical barriers are constructed, and people lose a bit of freedom with each. When they lose freedom, they lose the ability to use common sense, too.

Byron: How so?

Plato: For example, when a government enacts regulations intended to coerce individuals to act a certain way, it has good intentions. But government is most often too remote from the realities of everyday situations and ordinary people. The one-size-fits-all approach of government backfires by actually hindering progress. For example, a problem that is encountered by a worker can be solved very simply if the individual is permitted to be free to use common sense and his own individual abilities. But because a government regulation forces him to follow a strict, rigid, and cumbersome rule—unnecessary in this instance—straining against the stream of common sense, he must suffocate his individualism, and resign himself to be a sheep, numbly following the established rules. He is not as free. He is blocked from using common sense. Progress is hindered. Allowing people to be themselves is what enables ordinary individuals to soar, and society to progress!

Byron: Years ago when my brother was a corpsman on a navy aircraft carrier, there was an incident where a bag of medical waste washed ashore and littered a beach with syringes, gauze, and other things. In the panic that set in, regulations were enacted from Washington that shot down common sense. It became a requirement that from that day forth, *all* wastes generated from within the medical department of the ship be sterilized first before disposal. The intent was to prevent people from later coming into contact with wastes that were potentially infectious with viruses or bacteria. The intent was good, but the regulation that all waste be treated in a specific, rigid manner was excessive, slowing progress greatly. They were spending the good part of each day sterilizing even coffee grounds and candy wrappers, things that were obviously not infectious, while the medical personnel were taken away from their primary role of providing health care.

Plato: Yes, progress on the ship was hindered. I'll give another example of the failure of excessive external control: the disintegration of the Soviet Union. Too much government control over the lives of the individuals.

Byron: Individualism was suppressed.

Plato: You miss out on the power each individual could provide if he or she was freer and allowed to use common sense and his own judgment, which would generate real progress.

Byron: And when you have to pay before you pump at the gas station, you lose some freedom. Even though I'm not going to pump and run without paying, I am punished by having to spend extra time entering the store to deposit money, returning to the car to pump the gas, and then entering again to get the receipt and change.

Plato: And time adds up. The more external controls like this in the course of each day, the less free time you have. You are not as free anymore.

Byron: And internal control cuts your costs and increases freedom?

Plato: Certainly. Think of all the regulations required to run an unruly high school where the vast majority of students needed to be pushed and did not want to learn, and needed to be incessantly and heavily monitored for cheating. Compare progress in that school with the running of a disciplined high school in which students were self-motivated and wanted to learn, and only had to be lightly monitored for cheating. They regulate themselves with internal control, and thus diminish the need for the heavy-handed external controls that were a necessity at the unruly school. Much greater progress in learning is made possible.

Byron: So a greater reliance on internal control would be more cost-effective and efficient, and would allow greater personal freedom?

Plato: Exactly. It was Kant who claimed that even in a group of devils you could create a good society simply by organizing properly. Justice in that community, he explained, was a question of structural organization, which includes the use of external controls. But these are superficial solutions that, although helpful and necessary, are leaned on too heavily, becoming a crutch. We need instead to rely upon something deeper within each human being. In contrast to Kant, it was George Washington who said, in his Farewell Address, that in order for Americans to continue having the privilege of being allowed to self-govern themselves, they needed "virtuous" people throughout the land; otherwise they would slip into chaos and failure. The republic would not stand without internal control dominating. By virtuous, he meant people who were more inclined to at least strive to control their behavior from within, guided by universal values. A society founded solely upon an emphasis on external control was a weak eggshell of a society, vulnerable to fracture. When you try to keep people in line only by a legal system, by a vast collection of laws intended to regulate human behavior, you walk a precarious path.

Again, I plead the case for us all to rely instead upon something deeper within each human being.

Byron: But, you know, we need external controls more than ever. Unfortunately, the reality is that as technology improves, so too does it become easier for one individual to cause greater amounts of destruction, thus necessitating even more external controls! Years ago, if an individual wanted to cause harm to other people, he would have to confront them personally, face to face, with a hand weapon—for example, a knife. Then when gunpowder was invented, he could be farther away from his victim. Today, an explosive device could be sent from a distance, the person pulling the trigger never having to directly face his victim. And these bombs are employing greater firepower now than ever before. Can you imagine what the future holds, when nuclear weapons become more refined and accessible? With only the push of a button, an entire building or entire city can be wiped out. So there unfortunately will always be an increasing need for external controls. We have no choice but to acquire more metal detectors, bomb-sniffing dogs, security personnel. Unfortunately we have to arrive at the airport much earlier than in the past, so we can be processed through heightened security. And yes, I see progress is slowed ... your day's schedule has to be very different from what it used to be like; much more time is spent hanging around the airport, standing in long lines ... time you could be more effectively spending doing something else. Perhaps we are less free, but unfortunately we need to do it.

Plato: Again, I agree with you. External control is necessary. But this form of restraint must be counterbalanced by even greater emphasis on internal control. If we become more reliant upon external restraints, we become even more enmeshed within a futile circle of distrust. We come to distrust more and more people, since we trust in the external restraints to keep people honest. If someone crashes his car into mine as a result of speeding way above the limit and kills my sister, and afterward expresses his mental anguish and apologizes to me about his error, I would be inclined to forgive him—if the world were such that one could truly feel confident that most people had strong internal control. For in this world, the individual who hit my car would suffer greatly for the rest of his life, his punishment for his error being the eternal remorse he would be forced to live with. This would drive him to reevaluate his life, and he would alter his ways immensely so as to refrain from repeating such a mistake again. That would satisfy me. But in a world where there is a dearth of internal control, I would be forced to sue him and prosecute him for all that he is worth and more, in order to elicit any remorse. Internal control lacking, he might superficially apologize to me for his action but then walk away, perhaps with a smile on his face, thinking to himself how lucky he was to get out of this one. Then he would forget it ever happened and get back in his car and speed again down the highway. A world with little internal control makes it easier for individuals to sue each other, to blame others for their own inadequacies, to mislead, to dispose of principles for the sake of convenience. If no one else is playing by the rules anymore, why should I? It is a vicious circle, only destined to get worse if nothing is done about it.

At last, Plato and Byron arrived at their destination. They proceeded to the library shelves housing information about the world's religions. Most of the books in this section were covered with a blanket of thick dust. Plato selected four volumes and sat down at a table where they could look out a window at a copse of white birch trees. Byron took a seat directly across from the great philosopher.

Onto the wide, smooth table Plato placed the books and laid out the bare bones of this entity called "religion," arranging the parts into a sobering perspective. They were about to disembark upon a concise and honest dissection.

ON RELIGION

Byron: And how do you increase internal control?

Plato: The first way that immediately should come to mind is by participating in religion, which is traditionally a system having much to do with internal control. Because religion affects how people behave from within, largely without emphasis on external controls, it represents a most significant form of internal control. Let us define a religion as a system of beliefs, ethics, rituals, and leadership concerning the fundamental questions of life, which unites members of the group and affects the actions of participants in a profound way. A religion takes answers to the most basic questions about life that disciplines such as metaphysics and ethics ask, questions we can call the "religious questions," and then packages the answers into systems that guide behavior. A religious system, a religion, could involve only one person or it could be institutionalized, involving many.

Byron: As I recall from my studies, the metaphysical questions ask about things such as the origin of the world, destiny of people after death, reasons for existence, nature of God, and concepts of the soul. The ethical questions ask about the proper way to act, and the relationship of human beings to each other, the world, and to God.

Plato: A religion just takes specific angles from disciplines like these and places them together into one complete set of ideas. So the religious person, whether or not he belongs to any of the established religions, addresses these questions and derives from the answers beliefs, rituals, ethics, and leadership, the four basic elements of a religion.

Byron: And so to participate in religion—to be religious—means to address each of these elements, either as part of a group of people or as an individual, and to then use the answers to guide your actions. You can probably safely say every person that has ever lived, that had some degree of mental ability, had thought about the religious questions at least once in his lifetime, and then had some ideas about how he should act. So any person could be "religious," under our definition, including an atheist?

Plato: An atheist addresses the question, "Does God exist?" by answering "No." He next addresses the other religious questions, filling in the blanks for ritual, ethics and leadership. He or she may then participate further by striving to live by following, for example, the universal values. If you participate in religion by engaging in a serious, genuine effort to confront these elements and then strive wholeheartedly to act consistently, not randomly, within the framework you establish, you are being religious. Each day is composed of multiple decisions being made on how to act, religion guiding you.

Byron: I see.

Plato: The philosopher, William James, wrote about how some people needed to belong to a group, while others did better by themselves. He referred to them as tender-minded and tough-minded, respectively.

Byron: Yes.

Plato: And all of these religious questions engage the "spiritual" side of man, the part of humans that concerns the most profound and fundamental aspects of life. The religious questions involve areas difficult to conceptualize, and therefore do not elicit easy answers. Over the centuries, humans have struggled greatly with the task of finding answers. There has always been a serious, urgent *need* of human beings to get answers and then create some kind of system that gives order to chaos and gives direction on how to properly act. When you combine this universal need with the great diversity of cultures that have existed throughout the world from the earliest humans to the present, you get a wide variety of very different religious systems. A culture is a collective term encompassing all the concepts, skills, arts, institutions, technologies and such of a given people in a given time period, living together as a single community, working together for survival. The differences in cultures throughout the world result from the influences affecting each over long periods of time, and include geographic, historic, philosophical, psychological, economic, climactic, and sociological factors, to name just a few. These influences, when considered as a collective, integrating whole, direct people to perceive life in certain ways, ways different from other cultures. These differences were accentuated eons ago by the relative lack of communication technology; groups of people remained isolated from each other, the sharing of ideas being limited.

Byron: Yes. The Neanderthals had a religious system. And the Egyptians, Sumerians, Romans and Greeks had religious systems. Primitive tribes scattered throughout the world had these, too. And of course there are the systems of the Buddhists, Moslems, and Christians. All very different from each other.

Plato: And all very much alike, as we will see.

Byron: Interesting.

Plato: It is from the very different nooks of the world with the stark contrasts in human culture that different religions have arisen, each seeking to satisfy the universal need to answer religious questions and give meaning to life. And today in the United States there are citizens who follow these religions (I include, Byron, general groups, but also some of their subgroups in this list, so there is some verbosity): Jehovah's

Witnesses, Independent Fundamental Churches of America, African Independent Churches, Grace Gospel Fellowships, Baha'i, American Lutherans, the Albanian Orthodox Diocese of America, Moslems, Buddhists, Christadelphians, the Old Order Amish Church, Church of the Universe, Church of Jesus Christ, Church of Jesus Christ of Latter-Day Saints, Church Universal and Triumphant, Reorganized Church of Jesus Christ of Latter-Day Saints, Core Shamanism, Deism, Falun Gong, Hare Krishna, Kabbalah, Evangelical Friends Alliance, the Wesleyan Church, Cao Dai, Santeria, Discordianism, the Vedanta Society, Christianity—the Roman Catholic Church and the Eastern Orthodox Church and the Protestant Church, Eckankar, Hungarian Reformed Church in America, Rastafari, Zen Buddhism, Kemetic Reconstructionism, Secular Humanism, the Presbyterian Churches, Polish National Catholic Church of America, the Pentecostals, Syrian Orthodox Church, Tsaoists, Hindus, Wiccans, Sufism, Tenrikyo, Theosophy, Theravada Buddhism, Yoruba, Cherokee, Vodou, Urantia Brotherhood, the Universal Life Church, the United Nuwaubian Nation of Moors, the Self-Realization Fellowship, Neo-Druidism, Neo-Manichaeism, Quakers, Soka Gakkai, the Nation of Islam, Lakota, the Hermetic Order of the Golden Dawn, the Rosicrucian Order, Mandaeanism, Shintos, Confucians, Zoroastrians, Jews, Baptists, Methodists, Lutherans, and many others.

Byron: A long list!

Plato: Yes. Now let us look closer at the elements of religions. Beliefs are the first element to explore. Why don't you follow along here (points to a page of a book entitled, *The Religions of Man*, by Huston Smith) and read some religious questions.

Byron: What is the Supreme Being?

Plato: Ah, yes. The belief in a Supreme Being. This is a very frequent, but not universal, component of religious belief systems. This entity has many different names, such as Shankara, Ramanuja, Zeus, God, the Great Spirit. For clarity, let us call this being, God. Some religions believe God is a personal entity—it looks like humans and has a distinct personality. While one religion believes this personal being is always loving and caring, another believes it could be mean and domineering as well. Depending on the religion, the Supreme Being could be all-knowing, or not. It could be omnipresent, or not. It could be omnipotent, or not. Some religions hold the belief in monotheism, while others the belief in polytheism. One polytheistic religion gives uniquely different personalities to its multiple gods, who then interact with each other, playing out their dramas, sometimes affecting humans as a result. Some religions have a Highest God who is regarded as the first among equals, while others have a Highest God who is an absolute ruler in a hierarchy of gods. There are religions that believe God is three beings actually combined into one deity. Some religions believe the Supreme Being controls people's destinies, constantly meddling in their affairs. Some believe God could intervene only on rare occasions. Other religions believe the Supreme Being is aloof from people, separated entirely from their world. Some religions believe this entity has no resemblance at all to humans, it being instead an impersonal physical force. Some of these religions might, for example, recognize a supreme physical power centered within a strangely shaped tree which is to be respected and not trespassed upon. Another religion might, for example, take this a step forward and believe there is a supernatural spirit, with perhaps some human characteristics, living inside that tree. Some religions worship nature in its totality as God, while others worship only individual natural phenomena such as stars, the sun, or particular animals which are comprehended as forces that influence them and are thus in some way worthy of being venerated or placated. A pantheistic religion believes God to be everything in nature. One religion believes the Supreme Being could be whatever you chose—personal or impersonal. You could choose to believe in and worship a personal god, for example, while another individual belonging to your same religion chooses to believe God is impersonal. Some religions believe there is no Supreme Being, while others believe it is not possible to claim with one-hundred percent certainty whether a Supreme Being exists or not.

Byron: Take a breath, man.

Plato: Yes, that was a long stretch.

Byron: How did the world get created?

Plato: Some religions give God the credit for creating the world. Some religions do not, instead giving credit to an entity separate from God. Some religions attribute the creation of the world to completely natural physical processes, with no personal being involved.

Byron (continuing to reference questions from the book): What is the reason for human existence?

Plato: Some religions believe God created humans for his own amusement. Others believe people have one purpose, that of seeking to reach God's level of existence by following his commands. And there are many other variations.

Byron: What is the relationship of people to each other, the rest of the world, and to God?

Plato: Some religions urge the striving of humans to rid themselves of this world, through practices of asceticism, for example. The body and the physical world are regarded as obstacles to the attainment of the level God is on, so humans needed to separate themselves from this earthly world. Other religions believed God wanted people to use his earthly creations, not to avoid them. Rather than remain separated from the physical world, people are to live fully in it and use it as a springboard to the next world, God's level of existence. Some religions believe man should act only as an isolated individual and not become involved with other people. Then there are those that believe you must become involved with other individuals.

Byron: Where does a person go after death?

Plato: Some religions believe if a person acted badly in life on earth, he would be cast into a place called Hell, a rather uncomfortable place. If a person was good, he went to a nice place called Heaven, Nirvana, The Highest, or The Infinite, to name a few. One religion believes a jiva, or soul, which is a supernatural part of the body distinctly separate from the physical body, enters the world by inhabiting a simple life form. It then transmigrates into higher and higher life forms. Eventually, after many reincarnations, or transmigrations of the soul, the jiva arrives at a human, where it now possesses self-consciousness, freedom, and the need for responsibility. When this human dies, the jiva transmigrates to its next life in a different human body. If the deceased human acted poorly during life, the next life the jiva experienced would not be as comfortable as the previous one. So each act a human directs upon the world has an equal and opposite reaction on himself later; this is the cause-and-effect law of Karma.

Byron: And these beliefs are to be found in books such as the *Upanishads, Bhagavad-Gita, Dammapada, Tao Te Ching, Bible,* and *Koran.*

Plato: Correct.

Byron: Yes, of course.

Plato: The second element of religions to look at is ritual, which is a formal, standard activity serving to reinforce belief and provide participants with what they perceive as a means of controlling, or at least affecting, their relations with other people, the world, and a Supreme Being. Rituals are a mode of communication, allowing people to express to God praise, gratitude, repentance, or to ask God for help. Rituals strengthen people's hold on their religion as they become closer to it and the other members of the group. Rituals serve to remind individuals about their religion. This facilitates progress by assisting individuals in their daily behavior so they may act consistently within a framework established by the religion.

Byron: (Paging through a book entitled, *Religious Ritual*) Catholics recite the rosary in order to communicate with the Virgin Mary, and this is the ritual of prayer. And during Easter, they greet each other with the words, "Christ is risen," another ritual. And prior to Easter, they engage in the ritual of abstemption from specific foods, drinks, and activities such as dancing. There is the lighting of candles and burning of incense, other rituals.

Plato: In Western Iran, dervishes of the Ahl-I-Haaq religious sect enter into a trance-like state induced by the repetitious reading of sacred texts to the accompaniment of rhythmic music, and then walk on red-hot coals, grabbing them up into their hands. They believe they get closer to their Supreme Being by performing this ritual.

Byron: One of the members of Thor Heyerdahl's 1970 Ra Expedition was an African Moslem. Despite pleas by the crew to be economical with the limited supply of stored water, he insisted on performing the ritual of prayer and cleansing required by his religious beliefs, using only freshwater—no saltwater, of which there was plenty on this ocean voyage! Every time he prayed, he needed to wash his arms, legs, head and face, requiring five times the amount of water needed by each of the other men on board.

Plato: Great example.

Byron: I read about that expedition a long time ago.

Plato: Yes, a wonderful story! There is the Christian ritual of the holy mass. And there are other very different ceremonies performed by other religions.

Byron: And I would think some religions worship the power or powers they believe in collectively, while others require individual worship through meditation.

Plato: Yes. One tribal group drinks the blood of a freshly-killed bull because it is believed that life and vitality are contained in the blood. This ritual is actually only a small part of a larger occasion in which the rituals of dancing, music, and orally chanted prayers are engaged. Another religion has a ritual in which all the unmarried females paint their naked bodies in many colors, while the men engage in brutal hand-to-hand combat. The man who succeeds in dropping his opponent to the ground is declared the winner and becomes privileged to pick a bride from among the painted women.

Byron: The third element of religions is ethics (Byron points now to a book entitled *Ethical Behavior Throughout History*).

Plato: How must I behave? How must I act? Ethics consists of a set of principles by means of which a person could clearly and consistently distinguish between right and wrong behavior, identify his moral obligations, and regulate his conduct. Ethics addresses the need of humans for knowledge of what behavior is appropriate, what behavior is to be emulated, what behavior should be listed in the religion's ethical codes, what behavior should be followed in the interactions between people and the rest of the world. For each person on our planet, each day is composed of making multiple decisions on how to act. Religion, via ethics, directs people on how to act, attempting to bring order to chaos, and consistency to random, erratic behavior.

Byron: Basic to most religious ethical codes are guidelines such as "Do not kill, do not steal, do not lie, do not cheat."

Plato: A value is something, such as a principle or quality, that is intrinsically valuable or desirable. A person has value. A thing, such as a car, may have value. A certain way of acting may have value—and this is the key to understanding how essential religion is to progress. There are certain ways of acting, certain behaviors, that are desirable among people who want fair progress. These are behaviors that would restrain the relentless pursuit of the perfect life. These values are universally recognized as desirable by people who want equitable progress because these are values that promote progress and do not hinder it.

Byron: And examples of these universal values?

Plato: The following are some universal values, urged by most religions, which promote progress: trustworthiness, honesty, respect, responsibility, courage, perseverance, compassion, teamwork, helpfulness, sportsmanship, tolerance, hard work, loyalty, friendliness, courtesy, kindness, obedience, cheerfulness, thrift, bravery, pursuit of excellence, integrity, reliability, prudence, cooperation, patience, self-discipline, humility, fairness, self-control, innovation, and others. The more that people in a society earnestly strive to act in accordance with these qualities, the greater the progress of that society.

Byron: It says here (pointing to the book) that the ethical codes of the world's religions are found in various sources such as the Sutras, the Eightfold Path, Jen, Chun-tzu, Li, the Doctrine of the Mean, wu wei, the "Straight Path," and the Bible. And what is meant by the fourth element—leadership? I see you have placed upon the table a fourth book, *Religious Leadership and Authority In the World.*

Plato: The fourth common element of religions involves the assembly of religious leaders—the priests and such. Someone is needed who specializes in dealing with the problems and daily machinations of a religious group. It is common sense that directs people to cultivate individuals who will work full-time dealing closely with religious activities and issues. In this way, they will be able to devote the necessary continued attention and accumulated knowledge and skill to the issues. The religious authorities are elevated above the majority of people because of their capacity to understand and deal effectively with spiritual matters. Their advice wins respect and helps the religion continue to flourish into the future by keeping it strong, organized, and efficiently run. The leaders serve a counseling role, helping individual members with questions they might have. The leaders motivate the members. They direct the rituals. All of these leadership functions serve to remind and reinforce the spirit of solidarity among members of the religion, assisting them in their daily decisions on how to act, thus facilitating progress. It is also to be noted that some religions address the leadership element by deciding to eliminate leaders. "Let every individual be his own leader in spiritual matters," they advise.

ON UNCERTAINTY AND APATHY

Byron: Now, Plato, why is it that, despite the availability and diversity of religions from which to pick, there seems to be a lot of uncertainty and apathy toward religion? I mean, for one thing, which one is right? Are any of them right? I myself do not know what to believe.

Plato: Yes, there is much uncertainty, confusion, inconsistency, and apathy toward the department of knowledge that deals with life's fundamentals and questions of how to act. This exists despite the great number and variety of religious groups, each addressing the complex and baffling metaphysical questions, each attempting to provide ethical codes that direct people's actions and thoughts as they set out to bring clarity and order to an otherwise chaotic world. More than half of the United States population belongs to some religious organization, but despite the availability of organized religion, there is an underlying confusion with spiritual matters.

Byron: So there's a lot of uncertainty out here, which can't be good for tipping the scale to internal control!

Plato: Exactly. Indeed, although there are many people who belong to an established religious group and who strive wholeheartedly to adhere to its beliefs, rituals and ethical codes, there are many members of the same group who do not adhere because they have doubts or apathy directed toward certain beliefs, ethics, rituals, or leaders.

Byron: Yes, I was raised Catholic, regularly attended mass, and received Holy Communion. But I could never get myself to believe Jesus was part of a trilogy or that he performed genuine miracles. I did believe he was a historical figure who was not supernatural, but rather an extraordinary human being who genuinely cared about people and deserved to be a role model. Would I be a hypocrite in calling myself a Christian while not believing the basic tenets of the religion? Shouldn't I go find another religion?

Plato: There would be many people who would answer an emphatic "No!" to whether or not you could be classified as a true member of the Christian religion. They would asseverate that "To be a true member, you must subscribe wholeheartedly to the beliefs based upon faith." After all, these represent the fundamental reason for creating the group in the first place. And it is from the starting beliefs that the rituals and such follow. But also realize there would be others who would argue that you can still be a true member, since the important point is the affirmation of the ethical lifestyle you strive to live. And so each group has to fight it out as to whether or not you could remain a member.

Byron: And what if you were Catholic but disagreed with that religion's policy of disallowing marriage of priests? Or if you disagreed with the policy of refusing the ordination of women?

Plato: Yes, there are always areas of disagreement within any institution. These conflicts get worked out with time. There was a day when certain religions justified human slavery, and there were members who questioned that belief and worked to change it. Realize that any organization has positive as well as negative characteristics. Members should celebrate the positive, but work on improving the negative, and not discard the baby with the bathwater. Only the incessant struggle of ideas, the candid intense debate raged by genuinely involved human beings produces answers to these kinds of queries. Individuals on each side of these issues will try to persuade as many people as possible to take their side, and thus the incessant struggle will continue until a satisfactory resolution is obtained. And this takes time.

Byron: There are many individuals who frequently skip from one religion to another, unable to find a comfortable niche. A relative of mine was once a Catholic, then a Jehovah's Witness, then a Hindu, and I think he's now a Wiccan.

Plato: There are people who do not belong to any organized group, but who have formulated their own collection of beliefs, rituals, and ethical codes. Many of these people firmly and consistently adhere to these; others are not as consistent and unwavering. Some come to doubt the soundness of their own beliefs, and begin to feel a loneliness in not being able to share them with others, as they would in a church congregation, for example.

Byron: There are many people who don't pay any attention to religious matters. They never give it much thought.

Plato: Perhaps the uncertainty and apathy is fueled by a preoccupation with material goods and other worldly matters that draws people away, allotting no time or desire to sit down and think about this subject. There is too much work around the house or social events to be engaged in. There are too many video games to be played.

Byron: Perhaps there are such degrees of uncertainty and apathy toward religion because of the unfortunate existence of a vicious circle in which people see so many others discarding ethical rules, playing unfairly, that they make the decision that they must be like them so they do not lose out. The growing distrust of others steers people away from religion since "If you snooze, you lose! I'll go out and get what's mine! Why should I restrain myself?"

Plato: Perhaps there is the uncertainty and apathy because parents have not told their children about religion. In order for a generation of people to carry on the traditions of the previous one, someone has to educate them. If you do not teach children, how will they know?

Byron: And society as a whole doesn't support religiosity now. It's not "cool" to be religious. Instead, uncontrolled hedonism is the way to go in order to be accepted by peers.

Plato: Yes, a current preponderant view is that religion is trivial. Many people tend to be openly hostile toward it. Religiosity is often insulted by many people. Religious beliefs are held to be unimportant and irrational. A prevailing attitude is that religion should not be taken seriously. Religious rituals are belittled. In the arts, media and culture resides a great distrust of religion. To be politically correct, you cannot make reference to religious beliefs when you speak in public. You are better off keeping those views to yourself. In effect, the religious come to have a split personality; talk and act one way in private, another when in public. They act publicly as though faith, religion, and rituals do not matter.

Byron: Then, in a way, individualism, a cornerstone of what it means to be an American, is suppressed.

Plato: There is inconsistency and confusion in the way the doctrine of "separation of church and state" is interpreted and applied. Teachers and parents are uncertain of what can be said in the classroom about religion. Town officials are uncertain as to what is allowed and what is not when displaying religious symbols in public places.

Byron: And why else is there so much uncertainty and apathy toward religion?

Plato: We have discussed how each religion addresses the religious questions and the four elements of religion. These things represent a common unifying characteristic of religions. There is within the area of beliefs, however, a particular aspect that makes each religious group fundamentally different from the others. This is faith. The answers to the religious questions are too deep-rooted for easy conceptualization or physical, empirical demonstration. They are answers not possessing proof, but speculation. Most of them cannot be proven by the present powers man commands. How can man know for sure whether God is personal or impersonal? He cannot if he uses current empirical means. So why do so many people believe in a particular answer? Why do they believe God is a personal god without ever questioning this belief? Why do they have complete trust and confidence in the validity of this belief?

Byron: Because they have faith.

Plato: Yes, the answer lies in the area of faith. Having faith means a person trusts some belief without questioning its validity. He has complete trust and confidence in the truth of that belief. Proving how God created the world, for example, is beyond human capabilities and would have to remain an object of pure speculation. But since the Bible, for instance, describes the process of creation to have happened a certain way, then people having this quality called "faith" accept its description as being the truth. From the religious questions are derived the beliefs of a religious system, along with the other three elements. But the beliefs represent the real starting point from which an entire system unfurls. They set the tone for the other three elements. Each religion depends on its beliefs for its existence. And, in most cases, trust in these starting principles is based on the possession of faith. To be a true member of a religion, you must have faith in its beliefs.

Byron: So, many people do not have faith; therefore, the uncertainty and apathy.

Plato: Perhaps many people feel it is a deed of immense pretension to sit back and adamantly declare certain beliefs to be absolutely accurate. They discern a precarious nature associated with the supposed veracity of many religious foundational beliefs. For one thing, they may say, people of today are basing their beliefs on imaginative, metaphorical writings which were designed to figuratively illustrate points of view not to be taken literally. Faith is needed in order to believe these texts are only meant to be read and interpreted from the literal standpoint.

Byron: Yes.

Plato: Perhaps many people feel they are basing beliefs upon the writings of the people of long ago ages who did not know what we are privileged to know today about many things. These were the people of the past who believed the dark, outside air was poisonous to their health at nighttime. These were the same people who believed in mermaids or in the efficacy of blood-letting. These were the same individuals who held vehement arguments over whether or not the world was flat. So, to believe in their writings, one needs a high dose of faith.

Byron: But even if you did try to hook up with a religion, which is the right one?

Plato: That is another thing that promotes an uncertainty and apathy toward religion: an inability to declare one as the "right" one. Eventually we may wonder if there is one single religion that is "correct" and "best," for with the passage of so much time and human thinking, one may think some great leader or intellectual would have devised an all-encompassing, absolute religion. Or God would have united us all with one religion. But this has not been. The truth is that there is not one religion that is "superior" to the others, that contains truths that are "above" the others. People who are aware of the existence of all the many and different groups may become confused and frustrated. Many are sensitive to the immense pretension required to avow, "My religion is it! The one true religion!" while there are so many other valid and beautiful systems throughout the United States and the rest of the world.

Byron: I can see where that would make a lot of people uncertain and frustrated with it all.

Plato: Or what about all the bad things that happen in the world, like floods and earthquakes? A great many people feel it is difficult to believe in a God worthy of worship when He allows such random tragedies to be unfairly inflicted upon innocents.

Byron: There was a truly wonderful person, a good man I knew who would help any stranger in need. He was camping and a tree fell on top of him. He died, and everyone asked, "why?" What God could allow such a thing?

Plato: That is sad, Byron. And those kinds of injustices occur all the time. Another thing that may influence people to shun religion is the amount and severity of destruction waged in the name of religion. One of the South African churches once upheld its belief that blacks must not mingle with whites, thus fueling the apartheid system. Wars are waged using the name of God for justification to kill human beings. "A Holy War is God's will!" and "We must spread the word, the truthful word, of our religion throughout the world in whatever way it takes to coerce other peoples into seeing the truth ... we must save their souls!" Human history displays many scars from these perennial wars.

Byron: We engage in bloody, savage conflict over ideas that are not empirically demonstrated.

Plato: Yes. I tell the *Tale of the Boxers*. Two men visited the city of the Darkeyes and watched boxers who were engaged in an ongoing bout. They were two bulky men pummeling each other ferociously in a regulation-size boxing ring. One boxer wore red trunks and had on red gloves while the other had blue trunks and blue gloves. "They have been fighting for centuries now," said the first man. The second man watched with much interest as blood splattered all over the ring. They really wanted to kill each other! And they would not ease up in their heated confrontation. They just kept punching away at each other.

The first man explained further, "The man in the red trunks was brought up to believe that the floors in Town Hall were painted red, while the man in the blue trunks was raised to believe them to be colored blue. They had decided long ago to fight for their beliefs, to stand adamant as to their beliefs of what color the floors in the town hall are."

The second man said: "Why cannot they just put down their fists for one moment and walk peacefully to Town Hall to look at the object of their disagreement? That would surely be the most sensible thing to do? They could settle the question once and for all, and put an end to the vast destruction they are inflicting upon themselves."

Then the first man replied, "They are blind. And all of their ancestors were blind, as are the rest of their families and friends. They are called the Darkeyes."

At that moment, the blind boxers started yelling at each other, as they continued to pound away. "It's blue, not red! You stupid ass!"

"How could you be so stupid? It's red!"

"No, it's blue, blue, blue!"

The two men walked away. And the Blind Boxers fought on.

PART SIX
BICYCLING TO THE OCEAN

Plato and Byron left the library, crossing the busy street at the corner. Halfway up the next block someone beeped a car horn and, looking quickly toward the road, Plato identified his old friend, Soren Kierkegaard, cruising through town in a rental car. Kierkegaard pulled over to the side and waved to Plato to get in. Plato motioned to Byron to come with him.

Kierkegaard was in a jovial mood. Plato introduced him to Byron, affectionately referring to him as "Kierkegaard."

"I never call him by his first name because that last name just sounds so magnificent. It has a crisp ring to it. Kierkegaard! Kierkegaard!" explained Plato to Byron. The three conversed for a few minutes. Kierkegaard asked if anyone was interested in renting bicycles to ride the few miles to the ocean and back. Plato especially liked the idea, as he wanted to stretch out and get some exercise after his bus trip.

"I know where we could get bikes," offered Byron. "I have two of my own that are in fairly good shape, and know where we might be able to borrow a third."

Kierkegaard responded, "Sounds great!"

Plato said, "Excellent day for a bike ride."

Kierkegaard, producing a map from inside his pocket, asked Byron about the best route they could take to get to the shore and back by late afternoon. Byron pointed to the map as he presented a straightforward itinerary. "This way will give us plenty of time," he said.

"Today," added Kierkegaard, "we have an exhibit at the Sheraton. In the lobby."

"Yes. Plato told me about it. I will certainly check it out," answered Byron.

They drove to Byron's apartment on Miller Avenue and entered a small side room where he kept his bikes. They checked the tires to make sure they were sufficiently inflated, and Plato oiled the chains.

To obtain a third bike, Byron turned to someone who also lived in his apartment building. Byron's neighbor, a frequently disheveled fellow who lived upstairs, had offered countless times to lend Byron almost anything one could think of borrowing, including a chainsaw, empty glass aquarium with a crack near the top, surfboards, golf clubs, sailboat, and a lawn mower. As Byron rapped on the neighbor's door, he wondered how this person could fit so many things into his small apartment.

They were in luck; the man was home. He looked like he had just woken up, as he ran his knobby fingers through his long thick matted hair. Within minutes, he produced the bike. Byron adjusted the seat for Kierkegaard, and they were ready to go.

Some would assert that on this day Soren Kierkegaard looked like a "real" philosopher, while Plato presented more like a "regular guy." Kierkegaard's countenance was adorned with a heavy, long white beard. He could impersonate Santa Claus at a moment's notice. He even had the chubby belly, so there would be no need to stuff pillows down his shirt.

Plato and Kierkegaard recalled past shared experiences. These were old friends who had been through a lot together since the mid-1800's. "Gottfried von Leibniz temporarily lost his luggage," began Kierkegaard, as he did a drum roll on his handlebars. "He wasted a lot of time at the airport. But I guess they were able to find everything after an extensive search. Seems some lady took his suitcase by mistake. Both had the same kind of luggage. Same color. Everything. Just didn't read the nametag."

They began pedaling. It was a perfect day for a ride to the ocean. The sun was shining and the temperature was eighty degrees Fahrenheit. A very light breeze blew.

Byron felt as if he was caught in some kind of whirlwind adventure with total strangers, and periodically felt like he should have just returned home. But he was curious and interested and, so far, able to trust these two new friends.

They pedaled past a spacious cemetery surrounded by a metal fence. The blue of the Piscataqua River, flowing toward the sea, could at times be seen beyond the grassy green of the eternal resting grounds, from certain vantages on the road looking down.

The crest of the hill reached, the three men coasted down a short distance, stopping to walk the bikes across an irregularly-surfaced metal bridge. Below was one of the area's many narrow inlets from the ocean. They could see fishing and pleasure boats moored to the right and left, thick trees lining the water channel's banks.

Continuing, Plato serendipitously discovered the battered sign with its graffiti message the woman he interviewed had once seen. Plato stopped for a moment to better discern it. Squinting, he could barely make it out against the crumbling paint, as it was nearly faded from view by years of exposure to the elements. It said, "THE WORLD IS AROUND YOU, BUT." The rest of the line was painted over by "Ramona Loves Chicky Chadbar." The billboard seemed long-forgotten.

The road became narrow and winding, and lined by tall trees with bowed branches that leaned so to be directly above the pavement, in some places actually touching the branches from the other side as if in a leafy handshake. In a few weeks, these trees would turn into magnificent displays of autumn colors.

The spokes spun round and round as the slim rubber tires traversed the black asphalt. Homes became sparse, often set back from the main road, partially hidden by the greenery of the large population of trees. The sun radiated downward, pollen circumnavigated the air and, occasionally, red or gray squirrels darted past.

Plato, Byron, and Kierkegaard emerged into a wide open clearing, then crossed over a low, wooden bridge. There were kayakers paddling about in the high tide. Later in the day, this same body of water would turn into a field of mudflats. Seagulls chirped and cackled from the sky above.

Soon, beautiful Odiorne Park was on the left. Several cars passed. A group of serious cyclists rocketed by them, traveling in the opposite direction, pedaling in unison, with only a tire-width of distance separating them from each other. Kierkegaard jingled the bell that was hooked up to his handlebars, and one of the serious cyclists cracked a smile.

The smell of the salty air was becoming more prominent. Suddenly there were no more trees ahead on the horizon, just a wide expanse of cloudless dark blue sky. On the right was the wetland, with its tall grasses and floating lily pads. On the road's left was a wall of an assortment of variously shaped and sized rocks and boulders, and miscellaneous sparse vegetation that blocked the bikers' view of the horizon.

Soon enough, Plato descried a crashing wave crest. The wild saltwater lay just beyond that rock wall. The view of the Atlantic opened up to them as they rode further along this ocean drive. The water was deep blue, slightly darker in color than the clear sky's particular shade of blue. The junction between sky and sea could be easily discerned, unlike some days when they blended into each other with no apparent border.

The men pedaled a bit further along the road's designated bike trail, fully absorbing the stark contrast between this ecological niche and the tree-filled terrain they had just left behind.

At a roadside clearing, the bikers stopped to take in the scenery and sip water. Two of the bikes were left upright, supported by their kickstands. One bike did not have a stand, so it was rested against a wooden post.

Byron tipped his head back as he gulped from the water bottle. It was refreshing. The sun propelled its hot beams downward, eliciting puddles of perspiration. A cool zephyr mollified the severity of the heated air surrounding the cyclists.

They sauntered to the water's edge. Plato removed his shoes and socks, and walked into the cold water, and declared it "invigorating."

Two joggers passed by on the sand and waved with their hands. Soren and Byron strode over to the far corner of the beach, looking for seashells among the large dark rocks.

In time, the three came together again, situating themselves at the edge of the high tide. Byron positioned himself with his legs folded in front. Plato stood a while, and then sat down on dry sand. Soren took a seat atop one of the huge granite boulders.

Byron ventured, "So who arranged your transportation to New Hampshire? Do you have travel agents?"

Plato grinned, "We made all the arrangements ourselves."

"Where do you philosophers live?"

"In houses, apartments, whatever."

"What do you do for a living now?"

"Lots of questions. Too long a story if we were to try to answer all!" retorted Kierkegaard, chuckling.

Byron snapped back, with a grin, "Yeah, but a lot of people would like to know … "

Kierkegaard laughed, "I don't think you'd believe us anyway!" He stroked his bushy beard and tapped with his fingers on a washed-ashore lobster buoy, performing some complicated percussion rhythm. This seemed to be a favorite habit of his, for he often interjected a percussive episode as he spoke, as if to accent certain points, demonstrating that his drumming was of the highest caliber—precise, clean, sharp and coordinated!

Byron left it at that, as all three of them laughed. This was followed by silence, as they gazed at the ocean. Before long, Byron appeared to be agonizing over something.

Moments later, Byron broke the quiet, speaking slowly, "One day, when I was in high school, I sat in my bedroom flipping through a short paperback about Mother Theresa. Obviously you know who she was. I fixed upon one particular black and white photo which struck me most deeply. The image was of a teenage boy who lived in an impoverished place. He had an innocent face, full of life. The rest of his body, however, was emaciated, his bloated abdomen screaming with illness. At that very instant, upon first looking at that picture, something of the most profound sadness immediately overwhelmed me, and I began to sob uncontrollably. As tears flooded my eyes and rolled down to my neck, I closed my eyelids tightly, trying to stop more tears. But they just kept coming. Nothing like this had ever happened to me before. *It's just that he was about the same age as me*, I thought. He felt so close, as if I could touch his arm and say something to him. I realized I could have been just like this young person had I been born where he lived. I just wanted to help him."

Byron paused, as he looked away from Plato and Kierkegaard. Then he continued.

"Even though I felt like I needed to do something—to help somebody—when I saw the photo in that book, I realize now that I have never since acted on that desire. And for some reason, I remembered this incident just now. Perhaps I did so because I realize how passionate you are (directing the comment at Plato) in your desire to help make a better world. And I'm sure you are too (looking at Kierkegaard)."

Byron tried again to recall what he himself had actually accomplished in his own life to help a larger cause. Perhaps he was being too critical, but he came up short of anything substantial, and he felt badly about it.

Then Plato said, reassuringly, "If you have been a good person, you have done much already for the world. And to stretch yourself more, I am sure the proper time will arrive when you will certainly act appropriately. Sometimes it just takes a while until something happens."

"It's true, Byron," Kierkegaard reinforced.

Then Byron laughed and began, "Out of all the people around here, why are you hanging out with me, anyway?"

"Because you obviously have some interest in what we have to say," answered Plato.

"Which is unlike the majority of people," added Kierkegaard.

"Yeah, but it seems I'm just like everybody else—rambling around over the years with no real meaningful purpose. I think that deep down I have always wanted something greater, to be part of something bigger, but really have not found anything. Maybe I wasn't looking hard enough, though. I don't know," replied Byron.

"Well, the fact that you are here now may just mean you are ready to take an extra step toward finding what you seek," consoled Plato.

The waves were getting higher, spilling their foaming white crests onto the shallow water before returning back seaward as part of the undertow. As Plato listened to the incessant roaring sound, unheard of inland, he remembered all those days he visited the ocean near Athens.

"When I went to the Greek coast centuries ago," Plato began, "it always made me feel as if I was in stride with the rest of the world when I stood at the saltwater's edge. So many possibilities out there, in that thought-provoking cauldron of energy, where myriad ideas emerged from the diversity of people living in foreign lands, to be inspected and made useful in the quest to understand the enigmas of the wide world. The ocean was almost beyond my comprehension, appearing to be endless. Whenever I gazed at it, it served as a reminder that the world was out there, around me, a much wider world than I could know if I was to restrict myself to the limited view of a person trapped in a small town in the valley of mountains far inland. Or in a boringly plush living room."

A man up the beach wearing a wide-brimmed hat and walking a dog threw pieces of bread into the air, attracting a flock of seagulls.

"And not only was the ocean vast," Plato continued, "but it was to be respected greatly, for it could be calm one moment, only to erupt into a dangerous force at another. It was constantly changing, just like the world. I recall the evenings I would watch the sun scorched, weathered fishermen return with the day's catch. I gained an appreciation for the strength and courage needed to survive the omnipotent challenges out there. Life was not meant to be spent lived in isolation of its realities, many harsh. One needed to confront these. The world was around me, and I refused to spend excessive time in the spa. And to survive on the ocean, any navigating sailor needed to be constantly alert and aware of what was going on all around him. One needed to be respectful toward that ocean. If you were not alert and respectful, a storm of turbulence and explosive ferocity could be soon at your doorway."

Kierkegaard began, "My parents used to tell me you could hear the roar of the sea inside an empty seashell. Did you ever hear that, Byron?"

"Oh yeah. My brothers and I would sample different shells to hear which one had the loudest roar," answered Byron.

"Does your family live nearby?" asked Kierkegaard.

"Yes," answered Byron. "My parents and my four brothers. We are very close. We do a lot together."

The man with the wide-brimmed hat threw more bread crusts into the air as about twenty herring gulls competed to catch them.

Plato, his voice peaceful but trembling slightly at times, began, "And when you gaze at the horizon over the ocean and listen carefully—very important to listen with care, for too many people do not tend to this—you would discern the voices of people who live in faraway places. Give due care to remembering that the rest of the world is out there and around you."

Byron looked into the distance as three cormorants flew by and a small sailboat drifted along the coast.

Plato continued, "Those voices tell desperate messages seeking to be heard, drifting in with the tide, carried on the wind; words translated from Spanish, Arabic, Chinese, Russian and all the other languages. They say: *Your unrestrained pursuit of everything you want has brought you deep into our lands where you have advanced beyond the proper and usual limits. Of this encroachment, you seem either unaware or unconcerned, but do you not understand your actions have consequences that hurt us, that deeply wound us? Do you think it fair to us when you, who have not lived for generations inside our lands, write the boundaries on our maps? Do you believe it is fair when you install, against our wishes, your own puppet rulers who work to benefit your own short-sighted interests, who terrorize and torture their own people while you turn a blind eye so they might remain in power, continuing to provide you with the things you want? My wife and my son carry the scars. My young daughters were maimed and later killed. Oh, the indescribable horrors. Blessed God, I cannot even speak more now on everything else that has happened to me; it is too painful now. And this is just my story. Think of how many more there are. How much more damage must you bring about until you finally get it? We beg of you to not walk away in silence, but to change your course. Don't abandon us. Think of us. Don't walk away in silence. Otherwise, what do you think we are to do?*"

Byron, understanding, said, "The relentless pursuit of the perfect life affects how Americans deal with the rest of the world … "

"Yes," answered Plato.

A foghorn began its periodic warning cry somewhere in the distance. The air was beginning to take on a hazy character, almost like a mist. The cyclists decided it was time to start back. Soon, they were on their way back to town.

They began the return trip in the same direction from where they had come, except that they steered onto Newcastle Island, where they had not ridden before. They pedaled past the golf course, the marina, the Wentworth-by-the-Sea Hotel. At the Commons, they got an excellent view of a lighthouse. As they rode across three bridges, they could see a Coast Guard ship and submarine across the water at the Portsmouth Naval Shipyard.

Suddenly, Byron gave out a yell as he rapidly swatted at his thigh. Something stung him without warning. He barely saw what kind of insect it was before it swiftly flew away to escape, but most likely it was a bee.

Plato knew the sensation, having been attacked years before in Sparta, as he rode his brother's stallion.

They kept riding, as Byron muttered a few curses, pulling his pant leg away to keep it from putting too much pressure on the swelling area.

Kierkegaard yelled over to him, "It'll sting like heck for a few minutes, but then it'll subside a bit."

"So much for getting out in the fresh air!" Byron complained. For a moment, he wished he stayed inside his stuffy apartment where he could have avoided flying, stinging creatures. But in the next moment, he just laughed and kept on pedaling.

PART SEVEN
COFFEEHOUSE

Plato, Byron and Kierkegaard arrived with their bicycles at a coffee shop, the Café Brioche, nestled in the central square, catercorner to the bus stop where Plato arrived earlier in the day. They left the bikes on the sidewalk, navigated around the crowded outdoor tables, and entered the café to get in line to place their orders. Plato got a lemon square and large orange juice. Byron ordered a regular coffee and blueberry muffin, Kierkegaard a tall cappuccino and almond biscotti. After their orders were fulfilled, they found a table next to a window, where they enjoyed a wide, panoramic view of the sidewalk happenings. Many people were out and about, meandering and stumbling along with their lives.

Kierkegaard stirred his cappuccino with a thin straw, and then began playing with the frothed topping, alternating sticking the straw deeply into the foam with lifting it up a few inches above the rim of the glass, tracing figure-eights in the air without spilling anything onto the table. Byron stared, intently watching the repetitive feat of dexterity.

Plato and Kierkegaard sensed that Byron held a genuine interest in what they sought to communicate. In fact, Byron, despite being skeptical, had become comfortable in the presence of these strangers, and would have to admit he had learned a few things from them.

A small candle was lit at their table. Plato drew closer to it, looking at Byron with a sober, serious countenance and, along with Kierkegaard, began an explanation that would bind the day's experiences.

Plato solemnly began, "Why are we here? I mean all these philosophers from the past? Why do we come here now?"

Byron raised his head.

Plato continued, "As you saw, we want to find a way to lessen the relentless pursuit of the perfect life so there could be as much fair and efficient progress in the world as possible. We care about the freedom experiment in America succeeding, but are concerned it may falter."

He paused, allowing his words to reverberate.

AGREE

"The first step that can be taken to accomplish this," Plato continued, "is for people to get out of their living rooms, look around, and agree that there is a hyperrelentless pursuit of wants, with all of its manifestations, adversely affecting them domestically as well as internationally. Roll down the car window and see the aloofness, see the disposable society, see the victimization, and see the decline in health. Acknowledge that there is a problem. And people must then agree that emphasizing internal control over external control is the most effective way to slow this down. As a result, fair and efficient progress will be facilitated and freedom will have a better chance of succeeding, not just for the betterment of American society but also for the entire world. You cannot get rid of external controls, but you could certainly push internal control to a greater degree than ever before. The more people there are who agree with these points, the better."

PARTICIPATE

Plato continued, "The second step is to participate in anything that has to do with promoting internal control. This may be a secular organization that touts universal values, or it may be a religious group. Historically, religion had played a large role in internal control and could be used to reign in the relentless pursuit of the perfect life. Under this scheme, it would be up to each person to find something spiritual on which to hold as he or she makes the journey through life, for there are many paths from which to choose. You may participate in an established religion or in one of your own construct. Either way, you exercise internal restraints by living within the guidelines established by these. As you move through each day asking yourself 'How must I act?' you are guided by your religious system. People will choose different directions in their participation, but all must be players, for the sake of restraining the relentless pursuit of the perfect life."

Then Plato said, "It is important that everyone participate. And if you find you cannot subscribe to any of the established religions—"

"That's where I am ... " interjected Byron, removing his spectacles and placing them on the table.

Plato nodded, saying, "As are many people. But there are ways for everyone to participate in religion. People just have to figure it out for themselves. Ordinary people have the power to do this."

Plato reached into his backpack, bringing out a manuscript.

He then said, "Here I have one individual's memoirs on how he coped with the religious quandary. This is just one example—out of millions of different and very personal ways to address religion and make sense out of the world's chaos. At a minimal level, this particular person had something on which to hold, something to call a religious home, with the internal restraint it provided."

Byron was very interested as he began to outstretch his hand.

Plato calmly motioned toward Byron with his hand in a "halt!" position and said, "But first ... before you read this, I'd like you to meet someone. I see now this is one of those serendipitous moments of perfect timing! Some people might think this is a Hollywood plot!" He waved his arm to get someone's attention across the room.

At that moment, Epictetus came over to Plato, tapping him on the shoulder. "Hey! How goes it?" he began.

"Good to see you again!" exclaimed Plato.

Kierkegaard extended his hand and they clasped in a handshake. Kierkegaard said, "Byron, this is Epictetus!"

Epictetus smiled and said, "Yes, we met earlier when Byron was walking with Plato." Epictetus nodded at Byron, then continued, "And I have someone with me who I am sure you'd like to know." He turned to look behind.

With that, a man of unusually great size appeared with a wide smile distinguishing his face. Byron placed his tiny hand inside the behemoth's strong grip, as they amiably greeted each other. This tall, sturdy man had an aquiline nose, furry eyebrows, and a five millimeter diameter wart fixed upon his right cheek.

"You can call him Hulky," said Epictetus, laughing.

"Great to see you made it here!" exclaimed Plato to the giant. Turning to Byron, Plato excitingly proclaimed, "I present to you the writer of the notes I was just talking about!"

With a deep bass voice, the big guy softly told Byron, "When I heard this book—*The World is Around You, but You are in Your Car*—was being put together and my personal notes were to be included, I immediately sought to obtain a copy for my own perusal. I was disappointed to discover my part placed too close to the beginning of the story, where the reader did not yet have basic terms defined. I felt this was a disservice to the reader because it seemed to me that this fragment would work better elsewhere, so I respectfully lobbied to get the section moved closer to the end.

After some serious arm-twisting, the involved parties inserted it here where you find it now, simply entitled *Notes*. This is where they stuck it, the author agreeing with me. The author wanted my memoir to highlight what he called a 'minimal, bottom-line foundation not requiring blind faith, representing something on which to hold as you journeyed through life,' or something like that."

"Okay," answered Byron.

Through his manner of speaking and body gestures, Hulky seemed to Byron to be a highly reserved individual, not one to boast about anything. There was a certain reluctance of his to be in the spotlight, but at the same time, a kind of resignation to the necessity of having to explain himself so he might be of help to a much higher cause.

The big man continued, speaking seriously, in a dignified way, "I shall like to remain anonymous in order to protect my family from any potential media distractions, but will say I was born in 1915 and died in 1989. I grew up on the rough streets of Philadelphia, worked as a meatpacker for a time, and then became a trucker for decades until my retirement. I had always been a thinker—that's what the guys on the loading docks joked around about. I remember after getting my first tattoo, I began earnestly trying to figure out my place in the world. Throughout my life, filled with scads of scars, as well as heaps of guffaws, I jotted down these notes."

Byron realized that here was yet another supposedly dead person brought alive again as part of this strange, but interesting, experience that felt now like some kind of an adult fable.

"For my own limited role," Hulky continued, "I didn't write the following *Notes* to attract attention—it was originally done only for my own personal contentment, and for my wife and children to see where I was coming from. In fact, my memoirs were intentionally buried with me, and would've stayed there if it weren't for these philosophers who took an interest in them. It is humbling to have them included in this book. I hope these words are helpful. I'll leave you alone now," he concluded, as he left to rejoin Epictetus across the room.

At last Plato handed Byron a few pages of informal handwritten notes transcribed in cursive on notebook paper that was stapled together. It was neatly written and legible, and was simply entitled, *Notes*. The author signed it as "Anonymous."

Byron took his time reading this. Plato and Kierkegaard did not disturb Byron. Instead they began conversing with some people sitting next to their table, mostly talking about the weather. Soon, Plato, having finished his orange juice, went to get a café latte. Kierkegaard persuaded Plato to also buy a chocolate-filled pastry, which the two agreed to share.

*

NOTES:

I say every person who has ever lived is part of one big Human who builds a road. As more knowledge is acquired, a new segment of that road is laid down.

Theoretically, the Human can continue to amass knowledge until it actually constructs enough road to reach a place where people would know everything, including the answers to the religious questions. That level is the Realm of Absolute Knowledge, the road's destination.

Does God exist? And if God exists, is God personal or impersonal? Is God the creator of the world? How many Gods are there? Is God aloof or involved? Is God found in one particular rock or in everything in nature?

When a human tries to prove the existence of God by the usual empirical, ontological, and teleological arguments, he always ends up with the conclusion that God may or may not exist. Not proved either way. Period. It is a mark of maturity to accept this verdict. The road has just not reached the Realm of Absolute Knowledge.

It is also a mark of honesty when we admit that we, as human beings, are limited in what we can know about this. If someone asks me, "Does God exist?" I simply must reply, "I don't know."

I cannot subscribe to religious beliefs based on faith, simply because I need to have hard evidence of indisputable facts, but at the same time please understand that I do wholeheartedly believe religion is essential to life, just as much as food and water, because it guides our actions and is necessary for any civilization based on personal freedom to survive. I consider myself a religious agnostic.

Besides the scientific method of observing and measuring, how else does the Human acquire knowledge? The philosopher of some early century—let's say Thales—lives his life, spending much of it thinking. As he manipulates ideas, he scratches his head and sweats profusely at times. Thales even reportedly fell into a well one day as he was walking and gazing upward, deep in thought as he looked beyond the immediate to things of larger concern! But anyway, he writes down his ideas, concluding that water is the cause of reality. He pens many other thoughts, too, and his words are deemed original and important by the people reviewing them and so are given a place of high standing in the history of human knowledge.

Thales' ideas then become available to the people of future generations, continuing to have significance when another philosopher—let's say Anaxagoras—enters the world and reads about them. Anaxagoras simply picks up the book and absorbs in a relatively short amount of time knowledge that took the first philosopher the great part of a lifetime of hard work to discover and organize. The second philosopher does not have to waste time starting from scratch grappling with those same ideas to the identical degree as did the first philosopher, who was a pioneer into that territory. He does not have to reinvent a wheel. Because of this economy of time, the second philosopher benefits by then altering or stretching the original ideas of the first philosopher. Anaxagoras develops his own conclusion that water is not the prime causer of all things but that "nous," or the mind, is. The level of human knowledge is expanded.

Of course, this example of the growth process of learning includes the great scientists, politicians, mathematicians, engineers, doctors, and brilliant individuals from the other professions as well. All contribute to new areas of knowledge, largely building upon what was learned before while throwing in their own ingenuity. As they say, "We stand on the shoulders of giants."

It is important to also realize that not all the knowledge we have available today is *absolute* knowledge. After all, we have not yet arrived at the Realm of Absolute Knowledge. Because of our limitations on the road we build, not all the scientific "facts" of today are actually absolute facts; much of what we regard as true now will change to be in effect false in the future. Think of scientific "facts" that were considered true in the 1300's but yet, with passage of time, have been proven false. For example, the earth was once firmly believed to be flat, but that was eventually refuted.

Our knowledge about the world constantly changes as humans learn more each day. The important thing is that the particular information that is regarded as being *true*—that is, knowledge arrived at via the best human capabilities available at the time and believed to be accurate—may perhaps not be *absolutely* true—but *relatively* true and *usable* for gaining "more correct" knowledge, enabling humans to move closer to the Realm of Absolute Knowledge. Humans build with present "truths," and in so doing, either find those to remain valid for now or in need of disposal as they are replaced by newer and "better" truths.

We have heretofore seen that some prominent individuals are able to greatly influence humanity because of their ability to advance knowledge, based largely upon their grasp of ideas laid down before their time, as they secure a place inside the encyclopedias, worthy of our note. These brilliant people deserve our praise and gratitude; as they absorb all the individual contributions of everybody else, they are able to go beyond what the average human being is capable of achieving. They have the capacity to assimilate the surrounding influences and then reflect these back in a meaningful way.

We must, however, realize that this economical growth process by which we "stand on the shoulders of giants" occurs not only with the great philosophers, scientists, politicians, and artists—it happens to you and me, to every man and woman who has ever lived on earth. In subtle ways, all the people of the present have gained something from every person of the past.

Take one of the very first individuals living on earth, perhaps a strong, handsome cave dweller, and understand that he acted and thought in certain unique ways, influencing the others who grew up around him. One hot, humid day, he influenced his friends when he smiled, despite the fact that everyone was suffering from the heat as they worked hard in the sun hunting for food. The smile was contagious and was never forgotten. It ignited their senses to form a lasting memory. People he influenced in this way then went on to do their parts in the daily activities of the society, each contributing to the growth in knowledge. Perhaps they would think of that smile in the future when the going got rough and they needed to smile. This they learned from that cave dweller.

In the instance above, I wanted to take a seemingly insignificant trait and show it to be all-important, which it is indeed. We gain the smallest things from each other. Every little action is soaked up in ways we often cannot even notice or comprehend.

I will next give a more readily apparent example of the knowledge-accumulating process by which common people influence each other: despite the adverse conditions and the fact that everyone else had given up on the unsuccessful hunt, the cave dweller came up with an original plan to enable the group to swiftly corner a woolly mammoth by using a new combination of distraction and stealth. He was able to rally the hunters with his idea, which was then carried out successfully. The whole group increased its knowledge about hunting, and would use this to their advantage later, on future hunts. So people learned a new hunting technique from the cave dweller.

The cave dweller also influenced other people simply by going through the motions of performing mundane chores at home or doing routine tasks while at work. If he also labored as a farmer, his toils helped feed others, who in turn contributed to the society's growth in knowledge. Perhaps the food he harvested may have directly fed the guy or lady who invented the wheel. Or it may have fed other people around that inventor, the cave dweller/farmer thus indirectly influencing the creation of this device.

So people were influenced by seemingly insignificant things like the cave dweller's smile, or by more apparent actions such as his hunting plan or routine farm work. After the cave dweller died, the people he came in contact with during his life still possessed a part of him: his influences. His actions, no matter how small or seemingly insignificant, had influenced the people with which he interacted. Subconsciously or consciously, some of that caveman rubbed off on other people, which in turn passed to the next generation ... and the next ... and onward. In a sense, he is immortal because these influences continue to be handed down from generation to generation. The people of the present own a piece of him. We have an intimate connection with the people of the past. We all carry a part of each person who came before us, whether we like it or not, despite the fact that many of them were real knuckleheads.

The common person, one not recognized by individual name in the history books, is thus very significant, for his actions and thoughts, no matter how small, affect every other person. These influences may be subtle or overt and occur at every moment of life. They influence world history. You don't have to be a celebrity to be significant. The small contributions of the common person add up to the success of the larger figures such as Mozart. We are members of the backstage supporting crew for the ones who are in the limelight. Overall, one may sense a binding relationship among people of the past, present, and future. We all have and will continue to affect each other, mostly in small ways that add up to larger influences.

By performing whatever it is each of us does for an occupation, and doing all the other things we do in the course of each day, we build the road. All human activity contributes to the world's accumulation of knowledge.

The better, more efficiently, we perform our tasks, the more effectively will the Human construct the road. Every worker is significant in this endeavor. Individual people are like cells in a body, each with specific functions that are essential for the operation of the larger body. When a worker is ill or fails to show up, the rest suffer since advancement in road construction is hindered. If I bang my finger with a hammer, progress will be adversely affected.

In addition, efficiency in the road building is enhanced even more when individuals are allowed to be free to pursue personal goals and develop abilities to the fullest. This freedom releases the power of individuals which then promotes advancement in the road construction.

And so by working more efficiently, we build the road faster toward the Realm of Absolute Knowledge, but the best progress in any endeavor also requires that individuals strive not just to be efficient, but also fair. This means being morally strong by behaving in accordance with universal values and restraining from unfairly pursuing selfish goals. It is unfair when we lie, cheat, steal, neglect the kids, or commit a violent crime against another person. On the other hand, it is fair when people take pains to allow others an equitable chance to pursue their desires. It is fair when humans are careful to consider how their actions affect other individuals. In a fair pursuit of wants, people desire that others attain their aspirations too, and their actions are carefully undertaken so as not to be unjust. They know that fairness breeds the greatest progress since it is better to have everyone pitch in than to leave people out. When Black Americans were treated like second-class citizens, greater progress was impossible since not everyone was allowed to participate. The Nazis considered themselves to have constructed a very efficient society, one that made much progress, but the genocidal killing that was permitted under this society's watch obviously did not allow its victims a chance to pursue their lives in a fair way.

Just as an individual person grows through various stages in life, acquiring knowledge and progressing in wisdom and maturity, from infant to teenager to adult, so too does this Human. As we saw, with each new bit of knowledge acquired and applied, the Human builds a new extension of the road upon which it walks. If the Human was to act unwisely or immaturely, waging an unnecessary war, for example, the construction process could be delayed or part of the road could be damaged. A setback to the world's accumulated experience occurs.

The more violence we unleash among ourselves, the less productive energy can be thrust into the pursuit of knowledge, wisdom, and construction of a better world. There will be more potholes in that road, thus hindering humanity's advancement toward the Realm. Our children will occupy their work time repairing the damage we have done, and this will detract from their progressing closer to the Realm. Imagine the damage to the road if a nuclear holocaust wiped out entire museums or rendered industrial how-to diagrams illegible. We are more efficient in the road building when we refrain from blowing up things and each other.

Why would anyone want to unselfishly work so hard to build the road when no one knows if there is any reward like a Heaven waiting for us some day? Perhaps because we are all stuck in the same boat here on earth, not knowing answers to the most profound questions about life, surrounded by incessant dangers like diseases and hurricanes. We are so fragile here. As long as this is the landscape upon which we must dwell, we should unite to learn more about this environment, for our own benefit. Out of a necessity to make things better, we are tied to one another. It angers me when I see innocent children have to battle leukemia, or hard-working adults in the prime of their lives become afflicted with muscular dystrophy. It's best to work together to improve our conditions on Earth, to try to make the best of this precarious, questionable situation in which we find ourselves cast. The more efficiently we contribute in a fair way to this undertaking, the better it will be for all.

Despite the grim picture I have painted, I possess eternal optimism. There are a lot of bad things and unfair circumstances on this crazy planet, but when asked if the glass is half-empty or half-full, I neither respond idealistically that it is half full, nor do I respond pessimistically that it is half empty. I respond realistically that it is both—half empty and half full. That's an honest answer. I am constantly aware of the negative as well as the positive in the world. I celebrate all the good, keeping an optimistic attitude, while never forgetting the bad things as I work to eradicate them. It is my choice to believe that despite all that is unpleasant and injurious out there, there is always hope that that can be defeated if we work hard enough. So you have to have a little faith—choose to believe the world is an overall positive place that has negatives, but negatives that can be surmounted.

To strive to make the world better, we build the road—with efficiency and fairness for best results. The more we learn about the world, the better we can make our living conditions. When we increase our knowledge about medicine, we are more capable of relieving pain and suffering from illness or injury. As we learn about parasites, we will be better able to protect ourselves from becoming infected. The more we know about the weather, the more we are able to take precautions in advance of a hurricane's arrival. As we figure out our interpersonal relationships, we can get along better with each other.

There is a beautiful, complicated and delicate balance of nature that exists, where an action in one place causes an effect somewhere else. Someone said, "a leaf of grass can touch a star." As we build the road, we can understand these interactions and apply knowledge more wisely to help our situation.

It is with awe that we may think of fish surviving miles below the ocean's surface in pitch dark, of the interplay between atoms in organic chemical reactions, and of all the other amazing things in the universe. Nature is like a beautiful piece of dynamic, ever-changing art that I view with awe. The accomplishment of the Creator, whether the Creator is a person, thing, or some force we cannot yet make out, is no small task. I respect this Artist's world as I strive to understand it better so our living conditions might improve.

And so, I have told you what I believe.

My ethical code follows the Universal Values, which are behaviors that tend to promote fair progress. I strive to live up to those.

My rituals are interwoven within each day's trivialities. To me, ritual is eating, exercising, and driving to work. Watching an opera at the theatre or listening to it while driving my semi, or pausing in the middle of some quiet, deep forest is like going to church. In fact, ritual is in everything we do. And when I engage in the ritual of fasting once a week, I refrain from eating to remind myself what it's like to be without the things we tend to take for granted.

For me, prayer is quiet reflection when I think about the people of the world and my wish for them to be healthy, safe and happy; when I mentally review how well I have lived up to following the universal values; when I reaffirm my life's purpose; when I am thankful for all I've learned, experienced, and acquired over time. Prayer is really an attitude adjustment that inspires me to go out into the daily shuffle with renewed determination, ready to confront the world with fresh energy and confidence. I then affect local situations favorably, which then transmigrates to more remote places, ultimately touching the rest of the world. Waves of influences are sent throughout the planet, positively stimulating it. In our own little ways, we move mountains.

If I were to recite a prayer to myself, it would sound something like this: "The collective integration of our current branches of knowledge allows the realization that the mind is limited in its ownership of the Realm of Absolute Knowledge. The world of the Unknown Artist elicits an infinitude of inquiry and, I unselfishly admit, it is our children who will further our possession of fact; the limits of their ability to accomplish this depends upon what we do today. As for now, I embrace the beauty of this masterpiece, cuddling a wealth of happiness from the enthusiastic awareness of its goodness and being ... and I realize I too am an integral part of its mysterious scheme. I walk with care and respect around the dangerous parts of the landscape, and if only a universal respect for this artistry would blossom, I am sure that elusive peace and maturity would settle as a loyal and adherent companion of life. Just imagine."

I realize it is not possible to directly love and embrace people who live halfway across the globe, people I have never met. For that matter, I realize it is not feasible to smile and say hello to every single person that passes by me on a busy city street. We do, however, touch them in indirect ways by respecting and loving the people who are closest to us in our lives. We thus send waves of influences that affect the people near us, who in turn touch others, and so on it goes. By taking care to nurture our immediate relationships, the relationships which have the most meaning to us, we indirectly spread our love and respect throughout the world. By concentrating on living in the best way possible on a local level, acting with good moral character and respecting life and developing our aptitudes to our fullest abilities and so on, we touch the rest of the world. As the saying goes, "Think globally, but act locally."

A final word: I feel an immense responsibility to the people of the future. They will someday inherit the road from us. We who live today must realize our limitations and that our children will inherit the level of knowledge that we have prepared for them. With this inheritance, they may further the Human's abilities. They will be limited by the amount of knowledge and other influences that we present to them.

Perhaps our most important purpose is to unselfishly work as efficiently as possible to prepare the way for the people who will live here after we die. When we leave this world, a part of ourselves always continues on in all the other people and things we touched with our life, and so we are immortal in that way. As our children travel closer to the Realm, we go with them.

Anonymous

*

Having read the notes, Byron looked at Plato and Kierkegaard with appreciation in his eyes. He was grateful they had shared this with him. It was very interesting.

"I like his images, such as the road and the Realm of Absolute Knowledge," said Byron. "Yeah," he affirmed, "Very interesting. Thank you for letting me read that."

Plato called the opera-loving trucker back to the table.

"Your memoir is really fascinating," Byron said seriously. "The images are wonderful. One question I have is—what lies between the road and the Realm of Absolute Knowledge?"

"What fills the space?" the big guy rhetorically responded, as Byron nodded. "Good question. When I visualize it, I picture open universe—nothing but blue sky. But, you know, I went through a phase for a time in which I envisioned thick jungle vegetation completely surrounding the road and filling the space remaining to the Realm. So I guess it could be whatever your imagination constructs."

"As we all can see," declared Kierkegaard, "the recording of history is often unfair. This man should qualify as a great contributor to religious philosophy. But his *Notes* didn't make it to popular dissemination. Happens all the time."

"So your *Notes* tell about what is kind of like your own personal religion?" Byron asked.

"Yes," responded the Religious Agnostic. "It sustained me throughout my life. It might also be interesting to you to know I also periodically attended a Russian Orthodox Church, which just happened to be in my neighborhood. It was a place where I loved the sacred atmosphere and the beautiful rituals and music. It was also nice to be able to hang out with others, who were good people sharing in that spiritual experience."

A coffeeshop employee interrupted the conversation as she requested that the tall man do her a favor and change one of the burned-out light bulbs high up on the ceiling. "If you could do this, I'd be grateful. I just can't reach."

Kierkegaard chuckled, giving her a hard time, saying, "Don't you have a step-stool around here?"

"Yeah, okay, we do," the girl admitted, a guilty look crossing her face. "But it's way in the back room somewhere ... "

"Give me a new bulb ... I'll be glad to help," Hulky offered, happy to provide assistance.

Within minutes, the young girl brought a replacement and the leviathan easily removed the old light bulb and screwed in the new. The corner of the room brightened. People clapped their hands.

Hulky smiled and bowed his head.

A middle-aged woman wearing a Che Guevara T-shirt spilled out, "Just like the Abominable Snow Monster! Oh! I love that show, 'Rudolph the Rednosed Reindeer,' you know, with Herby and Yukon and .... " Her voice trailed off as she continued to name the entire cast, getting some of the names wrong.

Someone else in the café immediately quoted from the cartoon, "Look what he could do!" referring to the moment in the cartoon when the Abominable Snowman placed the star atop the Christmas tree and everyone cheered.

"Well, unfortunately, I hate to spoil the party," interrupted Epictetus, "but I have to take the big guy to catch a bus so he can get back tonight. It's just the way it works out. But at least he was able to be around for most of today."

"Wish you could stay!" exclaimed Kierkegaard.

The anonymous author engulfed Byron's hand with both of his and, looking down from his great height into Byron's eyes, said earnestly, "God bless you, my friend."

With that, Epictetus and the Religious Agnostic departed.

RECOGNIZE

Kierkegaard enthusiastically continued, "The third step that can be taken to lessen the relentless pursuit of the perfect life is to recognize any common ground that unites us. Why? The blunt answer is: because any time people have something in common, there is a tendency to show more respect and restraint in their interactions with each other."

The hiss of steam releasing from the espresso machine could be heard from behind the counter. The café was busy. And although service was swift, there was still a long line of people waiting to reach the counter to place orders.

Plato, who maintained a vast knowledge about the United States, explained that, "Americans are made of many races, religions, and ethnic backgrounds blended into one civilization. And in addition to the diversity, there is also common ground that unites them. Common ground is found in the beliefs described in the Declaration of Independence, Constitution, and other documents. There's the belief in giving as much freedom as possible to every individual. The belief in the immense value every individual has. The belief that people have the right to practice the religion of their choice. Common ground is found in the legal system, which serves as a kind of ethical code, guiding people's actions. Common ground is found in rituals such as the playing of the National Anthem, reciting of the Pledge of Allegiance, flying of the flag, observance of national holidays, participation in the voting process, and so on. Common ground is found in an established system of representative government with its checks and balances, tax codes, leadership positions, and so forth. Common ground is found in the use of the English language as the universally accepted language to facilitate daily transactions. Common ground is found in the history of the nation."

Then Kierkegaard added, "We suggest that there is also common ground found in a universal mission. It is for Americans to decide what exactly that is, but it could be *to constantly strive to do the best to create an atmosphere of freedom that allows all people to accomplish personal goals and develop their own unique abilities to the fullest while they use internal restraint, thus promoting progress that is both efficient and fair.*"

"In short," added Plato, "*to strive constantly to make a better world by nurturing freedom but also self-restraint.*"

"Every individual has unique and immense value, and is on the same team in this endeavor. When we work together in our local relationships, our actions ultimately touch the rest of the world. We contribute in small but significant ways to progress, so that in turn our children may inherit a better, more honest and fairer world," said Kierkegaard.

Plato sipped from his cup. "When you are commuting to work in the morning, you can take a look at the other people who are also heading to work, and know there is a higher purpose you share, all of you being in the same club."

Kierkegaard concluded, "Recognize common ground. This helps a little to lessen the relentless pursuit."

Without warning, the small coffeehouse was invaded by a band of four musicians, brandishing musical instruments and playing loudly. The first musician to enter the doorway had green hair. The second had hair spiked into five different horns projecting upward toward the ceiling. The third musician, a woman, had no hair, but her scalp was painted half purple and half brown. The last one in was a guy with thick-lensed prescription glasses and a striped Dr. Seuss top hat. They were grinding out the notes of some exotic punk polka.

Many of the coffeehouse patrons, taken by surprise, finding themselves off guard, rose from their seats, looking as if they were caught in a bank holdup. One well-dressed woman stood aghast and just shook her head in disgust. The trumpet blared and the accordion moved rapidly through the bellows shake. Then the distinct vocals began. Some people shrugged their shoulders, while others scratched their heads. One rather corpulent middle-aged woman began dancing, twirling in circles near the cash register. A policewoman could be seen outside the window, on the sidewalk peering cautiously inside, ready to spring into action if the situation warranted it. The coffeeshop owner bit his fingernails.

Then the song ended and the band took a bow. A smattering of applause later and the passing of a hat for tips, the band quickly exited the building and everything returned instantaneously to normal, as if nothing had happened.

Plato sipped the café latte and took another bite from his chocolate-filled pastry. The smell of the various coffee brews and freshly-baked bread and confections filled the intimate room.

Byron laughed as he looked around the café, exclaiming, "Well, there you go! You were just talking about this being a land of diversity. We just heard some very unique music."

Kierkegaard, in amusement, added, "That was quite … different. Very interesting. Can't say I've ever heard anything like that before!"

Plato smiled and said, "And remember, in a land with individuals so different from each other, there is also common ground that unites us all. Everyone!"

"That's right." agreed Kierkegaard.

They all laughed.

Byron sipped his coffee. Plato accidentally bumped his own coffee mug with his hand. Just a small bit of the beverage spilled onto the table. The candle's flame flickered momentarily.

Socrates walked in, hailing them with a big smile and long, drawn-out hand wave. He forgot he was holding a lit cigarette indoors where the rules prohibited smoking, but then realized his mistake when he saw Kierkegaard cupping his hand over his mouth, pretending to choke. Socrates went back outside for a brief moment to extinguish the smoke, then returned, introduced himself to Byron, and sat down. He reported on the ongoing symposium.

"Attendance throughout the day," began Socrates, "has been okay—not like it's been jammed with people, standing-room-only; but not bad either. A fair amount of people have stopped by, a few asking some very good questions indeed. I presented one lecture on 'Learning from the Past,' which appeared to be well-received."

"Good to see things are working out," declared Kierkegaard.

Socrates asked Byron, "Did you attend any of the lectures?"

"No, I didn't," he answered apologetically.

Kierkegaard defended Byron and said, "Byron has been getting the information directly from us; mostly from Plato, that is. And later we are all going to see the exhibition booths."

Kierkegaard performed at least five and a half drum rolls along the tabletop, once with two coffee stirrers, the others with his fingers. He was visibly excited about the day's accomplishments and seemed to be grabbing and stroking his long white beard more than usual.

Socrates excused himself, saying he had some pressing things to do and would see them later.

ACCOMMODATE

Plato ventured, "The fourth step that can be taken to lessen the relentless pursuit of the perfect life is to appropriately accommodate religion in the public square. Also called the forum, the public square is the place where people debate public policy. To accommodate means to allow in, give consideration to, make room for. There is a place for religion in the public square; however, there are necessary limitations. When a society chooses to cherish internal restraint, it must also clarify the rules about what is and is not appropriate regarding religion in the public square."

"Now, I think I know where you're heading with this. In America, there is supposed to be a separation of church and state," offered Byron.

Plato continued, "Yes. Let's see how well you know your Constitution. From what Amendment does this doctrine of the separation of church and state come?"

"Is it the third?"

"No, the First Amendment, which is divided into several clauses, the first two of which address religion. These first two clauses state: Congress shall make no law respecting an establishment of religion (the Establishment Clause), or prohibiting the free exercise thereof (the Free Exercise Clause). In other words, the Establishment Clause says that government must not *favor* any particular religion, nor *force* us to follow any particular religion. And the Free Exercise Clause says that government must *free* us to participate in the religion of our choice."

"I'll be back in a few minutes," interrupted Kierkegaard, grinning. "I see Socrates hanging around outside. Looks like he's up to something! Time for me to investigate. See you shortly."

Plato laughed. "Socrates has always been an annoying character, but I love him!"

As Kierkegaard departed, Plato continued, "Let's use the First Amendment rules to decide whether or not the following actions of government officials at work, and of public school children and teachers at school, are appropriate:

* A child, teacher, and senator wear a cross around their necks.
* A child, teacher, and senator wear a yarmulke.
* A mayor of a large city wears a turban on his head.
* A child, teacher, and senator read Bibles during breaks in the daily schedule. Another child reads his Koran during schedule breaks.
* A teacher reads from a Bible to high school students to illustrate how religious motivations affected world history. On another day, the same teacher quotes from the Koran for the same reason.
* A Moslem senator reads his Koran in his office every day, and sometimes quotes from this book in his public speeches.
* High school students learn in school about the world's different religions.
* A science teacher mentions that some people believe evolution explains the origins of humans while other people believe creationism explains it.
* A boy talks about Christmas during a class discussion when asked what his favorite time of the year is.
* A girl chooses to draw angels and a nativity scene in art class."

Byron responded, "I think these scenarios are probably okay in the cases involving children. But a senator or mayor or president—probably not good, but I'm not sure. Because they would appear to be favoring one group, when they're supposed to represent everyone. And the teachers—you don't want them appearing to indoctrinate the kids … ?"

"Actually," answered Plato, "using the First Amendment criteria, one may safely conclude that all of these fall within the boundaries of being appropriate. They do not involve the government forcing any particular religion on the public, or favoring one religion over others. And the government is not prohibiting anyone from participating in the religion of his choice. Just because a senator wears a yarmulke while he gives a public speech does not mean he is trying to indoctrinate the public to follow his religion. He is not forcing Judaism on us. He is not favoring this religion over other religions as he promotes public policy. He is just being himself."

Byron nodded.

Plato continued, "In fact, religious views, expressed directly or indirectly, are an integral part of public debate. Religion, as we have already seen, is a subject that deals with life's most fundamental questions, including the ethical question, 'How must I act?' The religious person addresses these questions and forms a belief system which affects his life's actions in a profound way. Then by participating in religion, he engages in a serious, genuine effort to strive wholeheartedly to act consistently, not randomly, within this established framework. Each day is composed of multiple decisions being made on how to act, religion guiding him. When a senator makes a political decision, he is obviously influenced by his religion since it tells him 'How must I act?' as he tries to use the best judgment and make the best possible decisions for the good of the society. If he did not acknowledge the role of his deepest beliefs about life in his political decision-making, he would not be himself."

Byron continued listening.

"And yet, because of the uncertainty and confusion toward religion, children have been penalized for wearing outward signs of their religiosity, such as yarmulkes or crosses around their necks. Children and teachers have been ordered to remove their holy books such as Bibles and Korans from the premises because of the perceived danger that others might be exposed to them. Children have been told, 'Do not say the word *Christmas* in this classroom.' It has been reported that children have had to cross out the word *God* from a phonics text, treating this word as if it did not exist as a word. A teacher in Colorado was instructed to remove books on Christianity he had added to the classroom library, while books on other religions—occult, Native Americans, Hinduism—were allowed to remain. There is confusion out there in the public square."

Byron followed Plato closely.

"It *would* be inappropriate if a school that allows students to wear crosses did not allow the wearing of yarmulkes. They would be favoring one religion over another, and they would not be allowing Jewish children to be free to participate in their religion. It *would* be inappropriate if a school did not permit a child to read the Koran while it permitted another student to read a Bible. And using Bible excerpts to illustrate how religious motivations affected world history is just being truthful in explaining what has happened in the world. It *would* be inappropriate if a teacher went beyond this by moving to a level that began to take on the appearance of actual indoctrination. He would be in violation of the First Amendment if, for example, he was leading the children in a daily reading from the Bible. How would you feel if you were a child from a different religious background as you stood by each day feeling inferior or left out while the rest of your classmates prayed in a way that was foreign to you?"

Byron glanced over toward the opposite wall to stretch out his neck and, as he turned to look again at Kierkegaard, he suddenly whipped his head back again away from the philosopher so he could see who was sitting over there. It was the guy with the cell phone, whom he had seen a few times earlier in the day. He sat at the table and was talking, rapidly and loudly, on the phone. And, sitting across from him was the little girl. But she was not drawing angels or playing with action figures. By now, she looked exhausted as she kept banging her head on the tabletop, switching sides from her right ear to the left ear, with her arms outstretched and her eyes rolling, an empty glass of Coke nearby, the ice cubes melted.

"Man, someone should probably disconnect that phone," said Byron. "Geez, give it a rest!"

Plato glanced over. "He's been at it a while, huh?"

They paused a moment, and then returned to their conversation.

"Now, it seems to me," said Byron, "there must be some limitations as to how much religion can be accommodated. There must be, to a certain degree, restrictions on religious freedom, as there are on any of our freedoms. You know, like even though we have freedom of speech, it's just not appropriate to yell 'Fire!' in a crowded theatre when there's no fire."

"You are correct," affirmed Plato. "A school may require students to remove any crosses from their bodies when participating in contact sports, for reasons of safety. A child would not be permitted to read a Koran at inappropriate times, such as when there are assignments to be done."

Byron added, "Those examples make common sense. But there are more complex situations out there. What about the Mormons and their belief in polygamy? Government perceived this as a potential disruption to the order in society in the late 1800's because it conflicted with the state and so this practice was ruled illegal. What about a Jehovah's Witness family rejecting medical care for a dying family member because its religious beliefs prohibit this? That conflicts with the secular culture's values. What about a Moslem landlord refusing to rent his apartment to a practicing Satanist? Or a Protestant landlord refusing to rent to an unmarried couple? These conflict with antidiscriminatory laws, I think. What about a Native American religion in Oregon that uses the illegal drug peyote as part of its rituals?"

"Yes, indeed," Plato said. "The state has its own secular values that will come into conflict with religious values from time to time. The question becomes, 'How far can a government go in regulating the beliefs of private religious groups?' We have already seen how a state would benefit by not hindering religions. How far can a government go in its attempts to force its own secular values upon private religious groups? What do you do if a child enrolls in your school whose parents claimed the family belonged to some religion that held as one of its rituals a twenty-day holiday in October during which time the child would not be permitted by the parents to attend school during the weekdays? If government is to honor this family's sacred belief in order to promote internal control for the sake of the society's overall progress, how is the child going to make up for the lost time from school? One school board member might suggest they hire a teacher to instruct the child in evenings or on weekends. Another member of the board would argue about where the money was going to come from to pay for this. The first school board member would then say, 'It is our duty to try our best to accommodate religion!' In the end, it may be that the board settles this issue by declaring this to be one situation in which limitations must be placed on the family's religious freedom."

Byron added, "This can really muddy the water."

"Indeed, you are correct. It is not always easy for the state to accommodate religion. There is always the danger that accommodation can take the form of differential treatment granted by the state upon a religion. A form of favoritism can be created, which is unfortunate and must be carefully monitored and avoided."

Plato gained momentum, as he offered more: "Just say that another religion comes along that requires the child to have twenty snacks during the course of a schoolday. This would be extremely disruptive to the class. But at the same time, is it not the duty of government to cherish and strive hard to accommodate religion? For the sake of internal control and progress? What specific religions should the state honor? Should they honor only the long-established ones? Or should they include every brand-new religion that comes along? Or will this be an example of the majority perceiving this as a 'lesser, unserious minority religious group trying to impose ridiculous beliefs on the rest of us?'

The family that belongs to this minority group may indeed be profoundly serious about the ritual in question."

"I see."

"So it's not easy to decide on matters such as these, but these kinds of dilemmas must be confronted daily and more consistently in order to be fair."

Plato paused a few seconds to catch his breath, and then continued, "The Amish do not believe in sending their children to school beyond eighth grade. The government holds the value that children must complete up to a senior year of high school, feeling this is necessary for their development. The Amish maintain a different view of this."

"So if you were Amish, who do you listen to—your religion or your government? The Church or the State?" Byron added.

"A complex dilemma. And if the government allows the Amish to participate in their religion without hindrance—that is, to accommodate them—this may be discerned as favoritism of one religion over others."

"I see," said Byron.

"The Native American church that uses peyote claims it was performing this ritual before any drug laws were passed. Some people will argue against Catholics' use of the drug of alcohol during its ritual of mass, in effect serving alcohol to under-aged children, but yet disallow the Native Americans to use peyote. It would appear this minority religion is being unjustly discriminated against. But other people will argue, 'If we allow peyote, what next … cocaine?' Or they might argue there is a danger that a group of individuals in Ohio, for example, may get together in someone's basement and say 'Why don't we start up our own religion and claim that peyote is going to be a drug necessary to be used in daily rituals?' Or they might select marijuana. So what do you do?"

"It's not easy," acknowledged Byron.

"And I should now mention a special word on the word *god*. This word appears in public on coins (In God We Trust) and in the Pledge of Allegiance. Sometimes it appears in public speeches, such as when a president concludes by saying 'God bless America.' The use of this word in the public square is offensive to some people who do not believe in a god or to some individuals who call their supreme being by a different name. They sense that the government is favoring religions that have God as their supreme being. They sense an imposition of this god upon them, without consideration of their own supreme being. Maybe the society should redefine this word to mean whatever each individual person regards as his supreme being. It could thus be any of those myriads of possibilities we described earlier. When used in the public forum, the word God could refer to a title, not a name of a specific Supreme Being from any particular religion. Maybe it could represent, in addition, each individual's answers to all of the religious questions, and the lifestyle that is subsequently engaged in. It could represent a reaffirmation of the value placed by the society in the participation in internal control so that fair progress could be facilitated. It could be a nod to the essentiality of religion to the functioning of the society. It could represent a reaffirmation of our recognition of the common ground that unites us by freedom of religion. And it could represent a reminder of the historic significance of religion's role in the founding of the nation, getting back to its roots."

"So if a Moslem is reciting the Pledge of Allegiance, when he says the word 'God,' he is referring to the God of Islam, and also acknowledging all those other aspects of the word that you just mentioned. A Catholic is referring to his god. An atheist is referring to how he personally addressed the religious questions and arrived at the answer that there is no God," said Byron.

"Correct."

EDUCATE

The conversation shifted as Kierkegaard returned to the coffee shop, filling everyone in on his brief excursion. "Socrates wanted to find out where he could play the state lottery, so he asked some woman. After they got talking, he discovered she is the mayor of this city. Soon after that is when I joined up with them. She showed us the place where you get lottery tickets. The mayor is very nice. She was thrilled about the philosophers' visitation. Socrates eventually went back to his hotel room, hoping to be a winner later today."

"What a comedian that Socrates is!" exclaimed Plato. "And to think he was my main character in the dialogues. And what about you, Kierkegaard—I thought you got lost, you were gone so long," taunted Plato.

"Plato, I was just gone for a few minutes!" retorted Kierkegaard.

"Well, Byron and I covered a lot of territory," answered Plato. "In fact, now is a good time to move on to step five, which is to educate … to educate people about everything we have discussed here."

"Ah, yes. A necessity," said Byron.

Plato continued, "The society takes steps to ensure that the children are taught about this, in ways that are age-appropriate, of course. For a civilization's theme to persist into the future, it must be passed on to the children."

Kierkegaard added, "In addition, we adults need to be periodically reminded of these ideas, so we may move forward with reinforced purpose."

Byron agreed.

Plato summarized, "Thus, all Americans would be on the same page. They would understand the definitions of fair and efficient progress, the freedom experiment, the relentless pursuit of the perfect life, internal and external control and their relationship to freedom, and what it means to appropriately accommodate religion. They would be united with a common mission."

Plato, Kierkegaard and Byron, sitting at the table, with the candle still burning, traded glances with each other as they realized just what this day had meant.

Plato concluded, "And so, we have tried to find a way to lessen the relentless pursuit of the perfect life so there could be as much fair and efficient progress in the world as possible, so that the experiment in freedom would have a better chance of succeeding. We, sitting here solving the world's problems, offering up our 'coffeehouse solutions,' have outlined five steps that, if indulged in, would create a genuine, sustained camaraderie and national purpose, would help us to return to reality as excessive comforts are shed and people get out into the world, would make us think twice about casual disposal of principles, would shine a separate light on personal responsibility in lieu of victimization, would guide us to live within our means as we hide our credit cards from our selfish abuse, and would motivate us to refrain from overeating, as well as from feeling inadequate if we do not have everything the people across the street have."

Then Plato suggested the three men go back to their rooms to get ready for the evening, when they would meet again shortly at the symposium.

At that moment, Zoroaster, Buddha, and Lao Tzu came in to the coffeehouse. Seeing Plato and Kierkegaard, they walked over to the table.

"You may have our seats," offered Plato. "We were just leaving. How has everything been?"

Lao Tzu answered, "Our accommodations at the hotel have been wonderful!"

"Excellent!" said Plato.

Zoroaster added, "We are taking a break from manning our booth. It's been fun."

The three historic religious figures were in a festive mood, very pleased with their visit to Portsmouth. Byron looked on in amazement, thinking how incredible it was to be encountering so many important people in just a few hours. Then Plato, noticing his wristwatch, motioned that it was time to go.

The three men left the coffee shop, returning the bicycles to Byron's home. Byron's neighbor was there to greet them when they brought back his bike. He asked if anyone wanted to borrow a sewing machine or a brand new inflatable two-man boat that was missing one oar. They declined and Plato and Kierkegaard went back to their hotel rooms, while Byron stayed at his apartment. They planned to meet up again in an hour.

PART EIGHT
IN CONCERT

Byron Dink found himself in a bit of a rush back at his apartment. After he stowed away his two bikes, the first thing he did was check his phone messages. One was from his friend, Beefalo: "Party tonight at Ed's ... just calling to see if you're going." Another message was from his mother: "Don't forget to iron those shirts the right way next time you wash them. Give me a call." Byron told himself, "I'll call her tomorrow." And he decided to forget the party—no time for that tonight.

Byron phoned his girlfriend, Angela, who was in Massachusetts with friends for the weekend. He conveyed his excitement about this adventurous day. "You'll never believe what happened ... " he began. Then he told her about Plato and Kierkegaard, the carriage ride, the trip to the ocean, and as many details as he could get in. Angela was just as excited as Byron, and felt badly that she was missing the experience. Byron told her before signing off, "Whoever these people really are, they seem nice. Very knowledgeable. You'll think I'm going crazy, but I almost want to say I believe they are who they say they are."

Byron remembered to watch the television so he could see if the philosophers made the news. Flicking on the TV with the remote control, he began cruising through the channels. The remote worked well for the first five channel changes. However, after that, it became erratic in the performance of its functions.

It would not allow him to go directly to the news channel he wanted, and sometimes it would not move up or down until the button got pushed a half dozen times. It was apparent that it was thirsting for a fresh set of batteries, which he did not have. Slapping the plastic device against his hand a few times in rapid succession, he managed to coax it to function properly again for a few additional channel changes. But this burst of success was short-lived as the remote returned to its incapacitated condition. Byron surrendered, tossing the contraption onto the far reaches of the bed and walking over to the TV set to manually manipulate the controls. He found the desired program, then lay back on the bed to view the news. He had already missed fifteen minutes of the program and nothing was said of the philosopher visits in the remaining half.

He began to fall asleep, but was soon awakened by loud music bellowing from the adjacent apartment. A song by Nirvana blared. The neighbor, a different one from the guy who lent the bike, was *cranking out the tunes*, thought Byron. Byron's heart raced as he lifted himself up from the bed, a burst of adrenalin pushing him to prepare for the scheduled rendezvous at the Sheraton.

He showered quickly, donned dark pants and a white dress shirt, and slipped into black dress shoes. After combing his hair, he wrote a short note on a postcard destined for his brother, telling him briefly about his day and that he looked forward to their getting together next week. He peered across the room at the crescent-shaped clock mounted on the wall, and discerned it was time to go. He affixed a stamp to the postcard, and then left.

At the Sheraton, Byron found Kierkegaard, as scheduled, who said there was a slight change in plan: they would meet Plato later. Some minor discrepancy had come up in the day's official events which Plato, being one of the chief organizers, had to smooth over.

Byron and Kierkegaard selected some of the food that was laid out on a long table for the exhibit guests. Kierkegaard introduced Byron to Jeremy Bentham, who happened to be passing through the dining line at the same time. Bentham told Byron he thoroughly enjoyed the friendly people he had met while in town and wished he could come back again next year.

As they carried their foodstuffs and made their way past one of the souvenir tables toward a place to eat, John Stuart Mill waved from his chair. Small talk ensued, after which Byron and Kierkegaard proceeded again toward a dining table. But as they traversed across the room, several more of the world's greatest minds appeared, as Kierkegaard politely made the introductions.

When they finally sat down to eat, Kierkegaard added a few drum rolls with his plastic dining utensils. They toasted the day's activities, raising up their paper cups of punch and tapping them together.

After they finished their light meal, Kierkegaard and Byron proceeded to view the presentations, which chronicled everything Byron had absorbed earlier in the day.

Looking around, Byron noticed there were about a dozen booths, each manned by one or two Great Thinkers. One booth was entitled, "An American Problem." Byron listened from the side of this display as Epicurus, his hair in disarray, attempted to explain to a small group of first-graders, in their language, how people want things but cannot always get everything, and how it is best to be fair about how you go about getting things. He explained, "For example, it wouldn't be fair to your mom if, because you only cared so much about wanting to play baseball outside, you kept forgetting to do your chores around the house or didn't listen to your parents when they told you to do something. If you are not fair and respectful of other people, then that makes the whole world not as good as it could be if you were behaving fairly and respectfully."

Byron and Kierkegaard moved to the other side of the booth, where they overheard Arthur Schopenhauer, his white hair sticking up like cat ears on each side of his head, discussing the manifestations of the relentless pursuit of the perfect life to a few interested adults. He explained to the onlookers, "So you see that each of these ramifications—the victimization, the aloofness, et cetera—drags down progress in some way or other."

"Yeah, I hear yuh'," responded one chubby man.

Byron and Kierkegaard moved to the next booth, which was marked by a small brown plaque that read simply, "Restraints." Lao Tzu, back from his break, was busy answering people's questions at this booth. Byron paged through brochures and studied various wall charts, like one that had sketches of the religious symbols from various groups throughout the world.

"Look!" exclaimed Byron, "There's an old-fashioned weight-measuring scale that looks like the same one Plato and I saw today in a candy store!" Byron peered at the now familiar device, wondering if it was borrowed from that shop.

Handing Byron two pamphlets, Lao Tzu explained that, "At this booth, we teach what religion is, what the four elements are, and how various groups differ throughout the world. And we teach how all religions are actually, essentially, the same. We teach how to participate in religion. And we teach the universal values."

"Yes, very nice," said Byron, lifting up a DVD about the Moslem religion.

Lao Tzu continued, "With regard to the subject of religion, teachers must not indoctrinate, as I think you discussed before. We can expose children to the variety of world religions, but must not indoctrinate. Secondly, it would not be appropriate to go into much depth at the lower grade levels because it is important not to confuse the children while their families are trying to teach them the foundations of their own particular religion. Teaching details and more advanced areas should be reserved for the higher grade levels."

Kierkegaard added, "It's not simple. For it to work, people must get together and come up with a consistent plan."

"The important thing," furthered Lao Tzu, "is that when you teach these things, people will be more confident about, more interested in, and more involved in the area of internal control; that is, self-restraint."

Another display was manned by Hegel and Machiavelli, both dressed neatly in suit and tie and shiny black shoes. Here, the presenters sought to answer the question, "What could we do to emphasize internal control?"

Hegel explained, "We teach people how to recognize the common ground that unites the diverse peoples, including the common team mission. People are being asked to write down what they think the common mission of Americans should be, with the best ones winning prizes to be awarded later."

"Wonderful!" said Byron, as he reached out to receive a free copy of the Constitution handed out by Machiavelli.

"And here we teach about the First Amendment," continued Hegel, "and what is appropriate and what is not in the public forum regarding religion."

"Very well done!" responded Byron, as he picked up a copy of *The Official Guide to Rules about Religion in Public Places.*

"When you teach these things, people will be more inclined to push the self-restraints that are so important and needed in today's circumstances," concluded Machiavelli.

That said, the overall message emanating from the exhibition hall was clear and concise. Many people were browsing through, studying the visual aids and asking questions of the philosophers. The symposium was a success. Those who attended were in concert with one another.

Then Byron and Kierkegaard departed the Sheraton, as they began making their way to meet up again with Plato so they could get to the Music Hall.

Plato was still back at his hotel room packing his bags, for by tomorrow afternoon, he and the rest of his colleagues would be gone. Tonight was to be the climax to their sojourn. He dressed and looked out the window of his room at the dimming sky. It was getting late and the concert would begin shortly. He put on his jacket, then left the hotel and began walking along the sidewalks.

He passed an alleyway where the smell of urine lay stagnant and a black cat sat atop a discarded washing machine. An ambulance broke the stillness with its piercing alarm of agony, pleading for traffic cooperation as it wove in and out of the road lanes, enroute to its destination. A baby began crying inside a lonely apartment building along the alley.

Night slowly began falling. Lights were activated, one by one. In fact, as unique as snowflakes, the sequence and rhythm of lights being turned on in the city was different each night. Plato marveled at the thought.

The lights accented the evening landscape, their varying colors, intensities and shapes defining functions such as stop-caution-go or Joe's Bar n' Grill. Some highlighted the windows of dwellings, the occupants within trudging through daily chores or floating along in leisure moments. Traffic lights conducted the vehicular ballet, while automobile headlights moved through the blackened air like coal miners with headlamps eerily walking in single file up from the depths of the earth.

Plato felt a kind of energy when he thought about how so many people were huddled very closely together within the compressed confines of the city. "Such a diversity of human beings, each having personal dreams and talents!"

As he looked at the many lit-up apartment windows, he knew that each would be an entranceway into a new adventure, with different and unique people breathing within. Inside Portsmouth lived a wide assortment of humanity, with every individual generating stories worth reading about and sharing. Each person was a sparkling diamond.

He was stimulated by a sense of the presence of such a wide array of ideas scattered throughout the city. People made it all possible. Initiated by one source, an idea would find another home and then begin traveling to other places. It would soar and then dive, darting this way and that, skimming along walls of buildings. A sharp wind would blow and send it in a completely different direction, perhaps swimming underwater or darting into another receptive mind. It could then bounce off a ceiling and tumble through an open window into the sky, its goal eternity as it struggled to disseminate and thrive.

Plato was well aware that gray areas in the arena of ideas were the norm, that black and white absolutes precariously teetered on the precipice's edge, but all sought to survive. He knew that even the concepts the Great Minds had grappled with over the past day were meant to be challenged still more, that their arduous work was unfinished, that what was required was the incessant battle of ideas. That was life.

Plato rounded a corner and spotted Socrates leaning against an Ionic column of some large ornate building. Socrates, who had been waiting for him, raised his hand in greeting and then took a drag from his cigarette. Plato smiled, "It is a nice night to be out, would you not say so?"

"You sound like a philosopher," Socrates answered wryly. "It's a gorgeous evening! I love this town. It has a sort of European charm to it."

Plato looked down the street. "We have a few minutes before we have to meet up with Byron and Kierkegaard. Why don't we check out the bridge?" He pointed to it.

The bridge's midsection was raised skyward when tall masts of boats and ships passed underneath. When Plato and Socrates arrived, a siren sounded and the bridge lifted to allow a large cargo ship to pass. The vessel had been out to sea for several weeks and was now readying to anchor at the pier a short distance further upriver. It was an almost eerie sight, such a large monster squeezing along the narrow channel.

The view from here was a classic New England scene. It had a moderately wide river, with several wooden docks jutting out from the shore into the swift river current. Dark-colored wood sheds were positioned near the water. Boats of all shapes and lengths were tied up, bobbing and undulating in place. Buoys marked various points in the river. A few unattended floating docks stood alone as if awaiting accompaniment. The naval shipyard ominously occupied the coastline across from the colorful floral arrangements of Prescott Park where couples were engaged in romantic ambles and seagulls mingled with city pigeons.

The Greek philosophers left the bridge and strode swiftly to a small souvenir shop where they met Byron and Kierkegaard. Socrates munched on a slice of baklava. They laughed over a newspaper story about a guy who lost his job and so began performing "stupid human tricks" on street corners. He had become a popular hit. It seemed his greatest performance, the crowd pleaser, was when he blew into his hand to produce a ripping, voluminous noise reminiscent of a chainsaw cutting through trees. Audiences rolled over in stitches during this act. In the newspaper, there was a picture of him in action, down on his knees, face turning red as he blew air into his hand, his cheeks puffed out, his suit disheveled.

There were other newspaper stories: since 1965, it was said the juvenile arrest rate for violent crimes had tripled; also tripling, was the suicide rate for kids, it was said; Scholastic Aptitude test scores reportedly dropped seventy-three points from 1960 to 1993; twenty percent of high school students were reported to bring some kind of weapon regularly to school; it was found that one-third of all high school students said they were willing to lie on a resume, job application, or during a job interview to get a desired job; in fact, it was reported in a survey of high-achieving students that eighty percent admitted to dishonesty such as copying someone else's homework or cheating on exams.

"Did the problem with the exhibit get fixed?" Byron asked Plato.

"Indeed it did!" answered Plato. "Just minor glitches."

Socrates, more serious than Kierkegaard and Plato combined, said in an almost pleading tone, "Byron, I hope, sincerely so, a dialogue continues forth … for the survival. It is very important. An ongoing candid discussion. We are counting on you."

Byron looked at the philosophers, an expression of gratitude lighting up his face. "Thank you, all of you, for everything! This experience has meant a lot to me. I will be forever grateful!"

Byron also, to himself, fidgeted nervously with the question of what he would now do with this new information. Was he up to a challenge? Did he even have the desire?

Byron interjected, "You know that what we talked about represents ideals, and it does now make sense to me. But I look about and feel like the *real* world is hovering over and suffocating all the good intentions. Seems it might be difficult to get all of this to work, to get the general public to buy it. It seems it is a losing battle."

Then Socrates lamented, "I know. It seems all is for naught, at times."

"Take heart, my friends," answered Plato, ever the optimist. "It is true when one looks down at the earth from distant heights, he sees better the human errors and silliness that play out, and it is easy to criticize from that lofty place. It is much more difficult to work out all the bugs when you are down here with your feet on the ground. But do not give up hoping and working hard. We can do better! At first glance, this emphasis on internal control may appear overly idealistic, but if you stretch for these ideals you at least increase the chance that more people will subsequently come over to do the same."

With that statement by Plato, Byron felt that, yes, he was ready to push himself more. He could sense a big change go through his life.

Finally, it was time for the main event. The Music Hall was being readied for the performance of the Tenth Symphony. There was a great degree of excitement traversing throughout the town as the denizens awaited this culminating moment.

Some people were talking about the concert. Some who would attend would do so solely to make a fashion statement, while others would be there just to be seen in a social setting where they could make points toward future personal ambitions. There would be some who possessed a sincere appreciation for the music, who could understand the sweat and talent it took to pull off something like this. They could passionately feel the hours of practice, the lifetimes of study and sacrifice on the part of the musicians, directors, and composers.

Within a few minutes Plato, Kierkegaard, Socrates, and Byron arrived at the Music Hall. Jesus Christ chatted with Charles Darwin near the entrance, but interrupted the discussion when he saw Plato come in. Jesus shook his hand, said hello to Byron and Socrates, and then handed Plato a five-dollar bill he owed him. They laughed about something Socrates said, and then Jesus returned to his previous discussion with Darwin, who was now joined by Thomas Hobbes and Confucius.

"Mr. Kierkegaard!" exclaimed Bertrand Russell. Kierkegaard had wandered away from Plato and the other two. Kierkegaard, dressed in a dark blue suit, his white beard draped over a bright red tie, waved his outstretched hand. They chatted quickly, as they exchanged many words all within the span of a few minutes.

"Did you win the lottery yet?" yelled Darwin to Socrates.

"Lost," Socrates mumbled meekly and right to the point.

Plato led the way up the staircase to the ushers, who guided audience members to their seats using flashlights to read the row and seat markers. The four men sat down and looked around at the beautifully ornate interior. Some paint was peeling from the ceiling, but this was just a minor blemish. The fold-out seats were comfortable. Plato had heard the acoustics were wonderful in this magnificent hall.

The orchestra musicians were warming up, filling the room with discordant noises. Plato enjoyed this immensely, however, since he knew that soon it would give way to a very organized array of sound. There was a certain charm to be found in the dissonance.

The lights flickered to signal that the beginning was near and people began taking their places. Plato, Kierkegaard, Socrates and Byron sat together.

The mayor of Portsmouth walked onto the stage, settling in at a microphone placed at the center. There was applause and then she spoke a few words. "It is important for us to take this moment to be thankful for having had the opportunity to play host to such a distinguished group of people. It has been a great honor and we are sincerely grateful for what you have given us. We surely hope you thoroughly enjoyed your stay, enough to want to come back and see us again some day! Thank you again! Now, let's all enjoy the concert!" There was more applause.

The musicians returned to warming up. Then the first violinist entered the stage and the audience responded with applause. The instruments were tuned. Everyone waited with intense enthusiasm.

Then the conductor strode swiftly onto the stage. The applause was louder. When it died down, he turned and proudly spoke. "Ladies and gentlemen … may I introduce to you … Mister Ludwig van Beethoven!" With this, the audience went wild. They were not expecting the master composer to make an appearance. He emerged onto the stage from the side opposite from where everyone else had entered. At first he did not smile, but as the crowd became louder in its appreciation, his face lit up with exhilaration. After shaking the conductor's hand, he took several bows and exited the way he came.

A finely dressed lady sitting next to Kierkegaard nudged him with her elbow and proclaimed, "I must say the makeup people really did a fabulous job making that guy look like the real Beethoven!"

Kierkegaard chuckled and retorted, "Oh, but that is the real Beethoven."

She smiled, but then looked away with a puzzled expression.

When the applause finally settled, the conductor raised his baton and commenced the Tenth Symphony. At once everyone inside the concert hall was captivated by the swirling, pounding melody. It beheld a heavy tone, powering ahead in a driving allegro tempo. The strings started the movement in prominence, but within a few more measures every instrument was heavily engaged. The musicians worked hard, as was expected, for Beethoven demanded no less than a preeminent effort from all. They had to reach into their very souls to tap into any extra hidden source of energy they could find in order to perform this work of the highest caliber.

The second movement plodded along at adagio, as if the first had slammed into a wall and had to crawl to safety. There was a sad personality to this section. The cellos cried in a supreme sorrow. And then the big surprise arrived: the third movement was even more sorrowful than the second! Byron noticed a tear in Kierkegaard's eye. There were many in the audience who felt such a painful sadness that they too could not prevent their eyes from welling up.

Then the final movement began ... slowly ... quietly ... could this be more of the same? No, for soon enough the music erupted into an explosive mix of complexity and joy! An exuberant counterpoint served as an undertow, tugging and twisting at the melody's spirited force. An intense, dramatic crescendo nearly blew the roof into the air, lifting the listeners into a higher level of existence, a whirlwind of precious humanity!

Plato smiled at Byron. Plato knew that it was important for the people of the United States to acknowledge that they had encountered a vast array of problems throughout their history and had worked together to solve or mitigate them. They had many accomplishments of which to be proud. They had used their collective ingenuity and tolerance for freedom of expression and thorough debate to devise innovative solutions to problems. And despite the severity and quantity of difficulties they faced today, it was important to remind themselves that they *had* come a long way! All that was needed now was for them to continue this strong tradition of rising to meet the task and confronting their problems with firm resolve. Hopefully, this visit from the great thinkers would stimulate a more honest and more focused analysis and debate.

Plato thought about the children as he closed his eyes and quietly prayed for America and the world. Kierkegaard sat to the right of Byron, drumming to the music by tapping his fingers on his shoes.

Plato wondered what the United States would look like in a thousand years, whether it would be so completely different as to be unrecognizable or just slightly modified from its current characteristics.

The music exploded into an overwhelming happiness. This was a celebration of life! Beethoven had once again conquered the darkness with his eternal optimism. There were always favorable possibilities available in the struggle to rise above life's hardships and enigmas. The beautiful harmony drove to a towering climax without any verbosity. Abruptly, the final chord was struck, the audience rose swiftly to its feet in unison and the concert was over. A standing ovation. The crowd was wild! Kierkegaard slapped a high five with Byron, as Plato kept nodding his head. People were entranced as they smiled at each other and felt grateful for having experienced such a majestic moment in history.

The next morning, it was time for the Great Minds to leave. Byron, as well as many others who had witnessed the miracle, felt so grateful that these human beings had been alive in our world. One by one, the Great Thinkers disappeared back into the domain of history, and the people who were left behind returned to their normal lives, working to pay the bills and enjoying their living rooms and cars once again.